Provision and Progress for Two Year Olds

Education at SAGE

SAGE is a leading international publisher of journals, books, and electronic media for academic, educational, and professional markets.

Our education publishing includes:

- accessible and comprehensive texts for aspiring education professionals and practitioners looking to further their careers through continuing professional development

- inspirational advice and guidance for the classroom

- authoritative state of the art reference from the leading authors in the field

Find out more at: **www.sagepub.co.uk/education**

Provision and Progress for Two Year Olds

Chris Dukes and Maggie Smith

$SAGE

Los Angeles | London | New Delhi
Singapore | Washington DC

SAGE

Los Angeles | London | New Delhi
Singapore | Washington DC

SAGE Publications Ltd
1 Oliver's Yard
55 City Road
London EC1Y 1SP

SAGE Publications Inc.
2455 Teller Road
Thousand Oaks, California 91320

SAGE Publications India Pvt Ltd
B 1/I 1 Mohan Cooperative Industrial Area
Mathura Road
New Delhi 110 044

SAGE Publications Asia-Pacific Pte Ltd
3 Church Street
#10-04 Samsung Hub
Singapore 049483

Editor: Jude Bowen
Associate editor: Miriam Davey
Project manager: Jeanette Graham
Production editor: Nicola Marshall
Copyeditor: Carol Lucas
Proofreader: Nicola Marshall
Indexer: Chris Dukes and Maggie Smith
Marketing manager: Dilhara Attygalle
Cover design: Wendy Scott
Typeset by: C&M Digitals (P) Ltd, Chennai, India
Printed in Great Britain by Ashford Colour Press
Ltd

Library of Congress Control Number: 2013947837

British Library Cataloguing in Publication Data

A catalogue record for this book is available from
the British Library

MIX
Paper from
responsible sources
FSC® C011748

ISBN 978-1-4462-7426-2
ISBN 978-1-4462-7427-9 (pbk)

To our wonderful children
Nina and Libby, Jess and Tom
No longer two years old but still our joy and our inspiration

Contents

List of figures   viii

Acknowledgements   ix

About the authors   x

Preface: terrific two year olds!   xi

1   Successful transitions   1

2   An environment for learning   11

3   Communication and language development   23

4   Physical development   38

5   Personal, social and emotional development   56

6   Dealing with feelings and behaviours   66

7   Checking progress at two years old   77

Index   95

List of figures

Figures

1.1 Further reflection:theories and trends   9

2.1 The characteristics of effective learning   12

2.2 Further reflection:theories and trends   20

3.1 Further reflection:theories and trends   35

4.1 Further reflection:theories and trends   53

5.1 Further reflection:theories and trends   63

6.1 Being 'emotionally flooded'   73

6.2 Further reflection:theories and trends   74

7.1 Further reflection:theories and trends   92

Acknowledgements

Our thanks go to the staff, parents and children of the Kate Greenaway Nursery School in Islington, who allowed us to visit and take such wonderful photographs.

Also to Jude Bowen at SAGE for her support, encouragement and belief in us.

About the authors

Chris Dukes is a qualified teacher with over 20 years' experience. She has worked in various London primary schools as a class teacher and also as a member of the Senior Management Team. Chris has a master's degree in special needs and through her later role as a special needs co-ordinator (SENCO) and support teacher, many years' experience of working with children with additional needs. Chris has worked closely, mentoring, advising and supervising staff teams to work with young children as well as with other education and health professionals. She currently works part time as an area SENCO supporting special needs co-ordinators and managers in a range of early year's settings. Chris is also one-half of 'earlymatters' training and consultancy, is co-author of the 'Hands on Guides' series of books and writes for various early years' publications.

Maggie Smith began her career as a nursery teacher in Birmingham. She has worked as a peripatetic teacher for an under-5s English as an additional language (EAL) team and went on to become the Foundation Stage manager of an early years unit in inner London. Maggie helped to set up an innovative unit for young children with behavioural difficulties and has also worked supporting families of children with special needs. She has taught on early years BTEC and CACHE courses at a college of higher education. Maggie currently works part time as an area SENCO supporting special needs co-ordinators and managers in a range of early year's settings. She is also one half of 'earlymatters' training and consultancy, is co-author of the 'Hands on Guides' series of books and writes for various early years' publications.

Preface: terrific two year olds!

In this book we aim to celebrate the terrific twos and we hope to shed light on how practitioners can provide even the youngest children with both the nurture and the stimulation needed to fill a year of life with growth, wonder and awe.

The increased number of babies and younger children in early year's settings has brought to the fore front the realisation that two year olds have their own unique set of needs. Two year olds call for large amounts of personal attention from empathetic, patient and supportive adults. Two years olds have a natural curiosity, a desire to explore and an appetite for independence. Practitioners can make the most of this zest for learning by providing a supportive, safe yet challenging environment which guides and channels such enthusiasm. A place where care and the early years curriculum is intertwined to provide a seamless and holistic environment where young children feel safe, secure and loved, and where parents instinctively know that practitioners have their child constantly in mind.

The book opens by recognising that positive relationships lie at the heart of all successful settings and that parents and practitioners working together from the beginning will give young children the best possible start to their learning journey.

Photo 0.1 A quiet space to look at a favourite book

It outlines how young children learn and how best to create a warm, nurturing and exciting learning environment. It goes on to provide practitioners with information and advice on appropriate expectations for development in the three prime areas of learning, as well as pointing practitioners towards opportunities which encourage young children to flourish. Two chapters are devoted to the personal, social and emotional development of two year olds, in recognition of the importance of this area. Lastly, consideration is given to checking children's progress and meeting children's individual needs. At the end of each chapter there are some starting points for further reflection and suggestions for further reading.

We hope that you will share our passion for the terrific twos and all the many joys and challenges they bring!

1

Successful transitions

> **This chapter includes:**
>
> - an introduction to working with parents;
> - admissions, settling in and home visits;
> - attachment and the role of the key person;
> - focus on practice;
> - further reflection: theories and trends;
> - further reading;
> - Parent file: the key person and attachment.

Working with parents

The transition from home into an early years setting can be an anxious and emotional time for young children and their parents. For many parents it will be the first time they have engaged with any form of childcare or educational setting since their own schooldays. They will often have preconceived ideas and anxieties based on their own experiences and attitudes and each parent will bring something different and unique. While *all* parents of *all* children have anxieties about this, it should be noted that for parents of the very young, disadvantaged, vulnerable children or children with special educational needs these worries can often be magnified.

It is therefore important that parents/carers feel confident that their child will be cared for as they would wish them to be and that they feel comfortable and able to discuss any concerns. Parents also need to be encouraged to consider carefully all the choices and options available so that they can make the best decision for their child. Often this will include practicalities such as getting to and from the setting, other children in the family, childcare, working hours, as well as what a setting has to offer their child.

Just as every parent needs to be treated as an individual, so the methods of communicating with each parent need to be tailored to their particular needs and circumstances. While some parents bring their children into nursery every day, others are only seen on the odd occasion. Working parents or families of children with special or additional needs may have particular time pressures such as appointments, hospital visits as well as other commitments, so reaching out to all parents can sometimes be a challenge.

Parents and what they bring to your setting

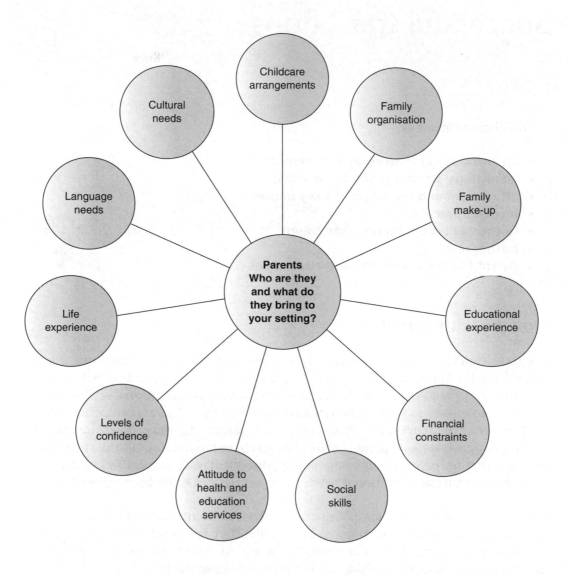

Childcare arrangements

Cultural needs

Family organisation

Language needs

Family make-up

Parents
Who are they and what do they bring to your setting?

Life experience

Educational experience

Levels of confidence

Financial constraints

Attitude to health and education services

Social skills

The term 'parent' is often perceived as meaning the mother; a father's role, however, is very important and their involvement is significantly related to positive outcomes for a child. While it can be a sensitive area, with issues around non-resident fathers or parental responsibility, it is an important question to address at your setting. All the staff need to feel comfortable about welcoming fathers, to emphasise their role, stress the benefits for their children and make efforts to target activities which encourage their involvement.

Working with families who have English as an additional language is also likely to involve a more creative approach to staying in contact. Using family members who can translate is sometimes the best way to overcome any language barriers. Care should be taken as, for some parents, there are issues around privacy and confidentiality when either immediate family or friends are helping in this way. Practitioners should be sensitive to this and where possible seek advice from the local authority or community groups who may be able to provide support.

Parents top ten worries

1. What if they become upset at separating from their child?
2. What should they do if their child becomes distressed and cries?
3. What should they do on the first morning?
4. What will happen if their child hurts themselves, feels unwell or upset?
5. Will their child be able to ask for the toilet or something they need?
6. Will their child make friends or be left out or alone?
7. Will their child be bullied or led astray by other children?
8. Who should they talk to if they are worried about their child?
9. Will the staff think they are being fussy or judge their parenting?
10. Will their child be safe?

Nearly all these fears can be avoided and parents reassured by careful planning and preparation. This is the key to good transition, whatever a child's age, stage, background or difficulties. The best settings are those which have a welcoming, well-organised and flexible approach so that parents feel able to discuss their child's needs before they start and can continue a positive dialogue which has the child at its centre. A 'can do' attitude is important, however, there are also practical steps which can easily be built into the everyday practice at your setting to ensure that every child has the best possible chance of a successful transition.

Admissions and settling in

It is helpful to have a written admissions and settling in procedure which both staff and parents are aware of. The fact that young children can take longer than others to settle into an early years setting needs to be discussed during pre-admission meetings and parents reassured that they will be supported for as long as it takes to settle their child.

Children cannot play or learn successfully if they are anxious or unhappy so the best settling-in procedures aim to help parents to help their child feel comfortable in the setting. The more information a setting has about a child the better able they are to plan a positive start for them and begin an ongoing relationship with their parent/s or carers.

Three of the best ways to gather information are to:

- have well-designed **admissions pro forma** that ask the right sort of questions. Settings need clear and detailed information about a child's needs, likes/dislikes, personal care arrangements, how best to comfort them, and so on;

- if necessary, and with parental permission, contact any professionals involved with the child or family. An **information-sharing meeting** can prove invaluable to the settling in process. Professionals can include health visitors, social workers, therapists, and so on;

- carry out a **home visit**. Try to build in time to make home visits an essential part of your admissions procedure.

Note: Home visits can only be made if parents agree to practitioners visiting their home. They can never be compulsory.

Home visits

Home visiting is one of the most valuable tools which practitioners have to ensure that a child starting at their setting has the best possible chance of a successful transition. It can be the start of a continuing positive dialogue which has the child at its centre, so building strong relationships and supporting parental involvement once the child starts at the setting is important.

A thoughtfully planned visit to their home environment allows parents to discuss their child's needs, can allay fears and leave them reassured. It also gives practitioners the opportunity to learn from parents how to undertake specific care tasks in relation to their child.

Details can be shared about the child's wider needs especially if there are health or other professionals involved with them. The setting too can provide information about the routines and policies, including the settling in procedure. A settling-in plan can then be agreed based on the child and family needs.

While it is often difficult for it to be built into the everyday practice of settings, as with all areas of pre-school practice, a 'can do' attitude towards overcoming the barriers is always helpful. Such is its value that those early years settings which manage to begin or have long-standing home visiting arrangements recommend it highly and are very reluctant to give it up.

Helping parents to prepare their child for pre-school

Many two year olds may not have been to a toddler group or any other type of group before. The bond between them and their parents will be strong and they may be worried about being left in an unfamiliar setting. Therefore, extra thought has to be put into how parents can best be supported to prepare their child for starting at your setting.

Some ideas to consider include:

- regular visits to the child's home by the key worker before and during settling in;

- encouraging parents to visit the setting with their child as many times as they feel they need to;

- agree a 'settling-in' period which encourages parents to attend the setting every day with their child building up to leaving for short periods of time until they are comfortable to leave their child for the whole session;

- discussion about setting routines and how they may be similar to home routines, especially in the area of care such as toileting and eating;

- a photograph album of some setting activities, rooms and staff for the child to look at these with parents or at home during the weeks prior to starting;

- contact with some of the other children who will also be starting or who are already at your setting such as friends or neighbours. The setting can help facilitate this by holding a coffee morning for all new parents/carers and children;

- attending drop in sessions and any special events that the setting may be having;

- share stories and books about starting at pre-school, consider drawing up a list of suitable titles to give to parents.

Photo 1.1   Role play with the key person

The role of the key person

Key workers who have responsibility for working with a child on a daily basis are in a unique position to also work with their parents. Not only do they get to know an individual child but they also have broader experience of a wide range of children, knowledge of child development, and a wealth of ideas and strategies for play and the curriculum.

The crucial role of the key person in the care, well-being and development of babies and young children has been highlighted in recent times by the re-emergence of attachment as a theory which underpins the work of early year's practitioners. 'Deep, long lasting emotional attachment influences mind, body, emotions, relationships and values, and has a positive impact on self-esteem, independence the ability to make both temporary and enduring relationships, empathy, compassion and resiliency' (Allen, 2011: 14 see further reading).

While a child's first attachment is most likely to be with its mother or primary caregiver, for practitioners, its importance lies in the effects that both secure and insecure attachment can have on the children in their settings. As a greater number of younger children are entering day care settings, nurseries and children's centres, the role of the practitioners in continuing to foster positive attachment is crucial, and the younger the child the more significant the role. On a practical level this involves a three-way process between the child, the parents, and the practitioners who are in daily contact with the child.

What is attachment?

Attachment has its roots in the work of psychoanalyst John Bowlby (1969) whose theory suggested that from birth, babies are instinctively looking for secure attachments and seeking to engage socially and emotionally. In order to have their needs met they seek comfort in being close, both physically and emotionally, to a small number of caregivers, especially their mothers. Babies and young children therefore develop best when caregivers respond to them in a warm, caring and consistent way. Secure attachment also facilitates learning as children are able to explore their environment and objects within it from a place of safety, secure in knowing that they have an attachment figure or base to return to. The quality of a child's learning and the development of resilience can depend on the quality of their relationships both with their key person and their primary caregivers.

Those babies and young children who have unhappy or unresponsive caregivers or those who live in an environment that lacks basic care, stimulation or love may have insecure attachment. There are many reasons why a secure attachment may not have been established, for example, if either the child or parent has been ill or separated from each other, this can cause disruption to the relationship. So too can post-natal depression or family difficulties and stress which mean that the adult is not able to respond to the child in a way that would form this attachment.

A lack of secure attachment can have far-reaching effects on all aspects of a child's development which can last into adulthood, so the importance of a secure, sensitive, responsive and consistent relationship cannot be emphasised enough.

The science of attachment

More recent developments in neuroscience, psychology and biochemistry have linked into this theory and enabled us to gain further insight into not only how the brain develops, but also how our emotions affect the brain and our social behaviour.

Brain cells start to develop during the first few weeks of pregnancy and by the time a baby is born it has 100 billion brain cells. While the baby is still in the womb these cells are already developing specific functions and connections, or synapses. One of the things that can impede the development of these connections is high levels of the hormone cortisol, which is produced as a response to stress.

Babies and young children can become stressed and release cortisol if their caregiver lacks responsiveness to either their physical or emotional needs. It is therefore good early attachment relationships which help children to develop the connections between brain cells that are needed for all future development and learning. This includes a child's emotional learning, and research into early brain development also identifies that different parts of the brain develop during specific windows of time. The foundation of a child's emotional development is estimated to take place in the first 18 months, so very early in a child's life. For example, empathy, understanding the feelings of others and how their own behaviour affects others, begins to develop.

Attachment – supporting parents and carers

Some parents can become anxious about their child forming an attachment to their key person. It can be viewed as in some way threatening to their own relationship with their child and raises concerns about who their child prefers to be with. The familiar scenario of a child who does not want to go home at the end of the nursery morning can be particularly upsetting for parents.

It is very important, therefore, that practitioners are able to form good relationships with parents and are able to explain the benefits of having secure attachments to a key person while stressing that their parents are the most important people in the child's life and ultimately their first educator.

 Focus on practice

Children are able to form more than one attachment and whatever a child's early experience, it is a process that those working in the early years can and should influence. Be flexible when allocating key workers. If the child and/or parent makes a bond with a particular member of staff, consider changing the key worker to accommodate this.

Babies and young children develop best when caregivers respond to them in a warm, caring and consistent way.

Make some 'one-on-one' time every day with individual children to help them feel safe and valued.

Children need adults to set a good example and to give them opportunities for interaction with others so that they can develop positive ideas about themselves and others.

Being acknowledged and affirmed by important people in their lives leads to children gaining confidence and inner strength through secure attachments with these people. Show genuine interest in the things children do and say, find out what they like and help to raise individual children's 'positive profile' with other staff and children.

Exploration within close relationships leads to growth of self-assurance, promoting a sense of belonging which allows children to explore the world from a secure base. Value individual efforts and find different ways to say 'well done' and strive to build positive self-esteem in your key group children.

Children who are encouraged to feel free to express their ideas and their feelings such as joy, sadness, frustration and fear can develop strategies to cope with new, challenging or stressful situations. Acknowledge and label feelings and emotions so that children develop the vocabulary to talk about them. Provide a safe place to go when things get too much.

The way children behave and achieve is directly related to the way they feel, and so for all children behaviour is a form of communication. For those children who are not securely attached it is even more so and often becomes a way of getting what they need.

Connecting with parents

- Make time each day to say hello and something positive to parents about their child. Let them know what their child has been doing at nursery and ensure that they also share news from home.

- Have a conversation at least weekly with every parent about their child (keep an informal list). Establishing a pattern of talking to parents about everyday matters will make it easier to discuss difficult issues.

- Listen carefully to what parents have to say about their child, acknowledge they know best and ensure that you respect child-rearing practices different from your own.

- Create opportunities for key workers and parents to meet more informally to build up relationships. This can be during workshops, coffee mornings, volunteer helper sessions, trips and so on.

- Keep the relationship friendly and supportive but maintain your professionalism. Be available to talk but make sure first you have the time; if not, arrange a mutually convenient time when you can prepare for a meeting.

- Make sure parents know what is happening in the setting by finding an effective way to communicate with busy people, for example, a noticeboard, a communication book, text messages, email, photographs.

- Tell parents who their child is friendly with to encourage play dates and support parents to get to know each other by introductions, coffee mornings and socials. An annual parent/child event such as a concert or a picnic can build good relationships and is fun.

- Keep a register of parent skills and involve them as volunteers and fund-raisers.

- Remind parents about agreements and issues such as payments in a way that is not public or embarrassing.

- Set up a small comfortable 'Parent space' for parents waiting or settling their children.

- Put yourself in their shoes. Sometimes it is invaluable to remind yourself and colleagues of how a parent might be feeling.

Further reflection: theories and trends

Neuroscience

Modern brain research has brought new insight into how babies and young children's first experiences and relationships affect their brain development and function. This particularly affects social and emotional intelligence and has far reaching implications for later life.

J. Panksepp

Psychoanalytic theories

There has been a re-emergence of attachment theory, for example. It does much to support the idea of a key person approach and the practitioner as a 'secondary attachment'.

J. Bowlby
D. Winnicott

Figure 1.1

Further reading

Allen, G. (2011) *Early Intervention: The Next Steps*. London: HM Government.

Brownlee, P. (2008) *Dance With Me in the Heart*. Auckland: New Zealand Playcentre Publications.

Dukes, C. and Smith, M. (2009) *Building Better Behaviour in the Early Years*. London: SAGE.

Gerhardt, S. (2004) *Why Love Matters. How Affection Shapes a Baby's Brain*. London: Routledge.

Holmes, J. (1993) *John Bowlby and Attachment Theory*. London: Routledge.

Lindon, J. (2012) *What Does It Mean To Be Two?* London: Practical Pre-school.

Mathieson, K. (2013) *I Am Two: Working Effectively with Two Year Olds and Their Families*. London: Early Education.

Miller, L. and Pound, L. (2011) *Theories and Approaches to Learning in the Early Years*. London: SAGE.

Nutkins, S., McDonald, C. and Stephens, M. (2013) *Early Childhood Education and Care*. London: SAGE.

Oates, J. (ed.) (2007) *Attachment Relationships*. Milton Keynes: Open University Press.

Sutherland, M. (2006) *The Science of Parenting*. London: Dorling Kindersley.

Recommended websites

www.workingwithmen.org

www.fatherhoodinstitute.org

The above are resources to support the engagement of fathers.

Parent file

The key person and attachment

Q. **What is attachment?**

A. Attachment is a theory which says that babies instinctively look for secure attachments in order to have their needs met and to seek comfort in being close, both physically and emotionally. A young child's first attachment is usually with its mother or main caregiver and once this is secure, secondary attachment to other adults is possible.

Q. **What does the theory of attachment mean for the early years setting?**

A. Attachment theory has prompted further research which has resulted in the key person approach which is now considered to be an essential part of early years practice.

Q. **What is the key person approach?**

A. The key person approach is a way of working which enables and supports close attachments between individual children and individual practitioners.

Q. **Does the key person approach involve me?**

A. Yes, it encourages a close working relationship between the practitioner and the parent or carer and recognises that parents are the most important people in the child's life and ultimately their first educator.

Q. **Should I be worried that my child has too close an attachment to the key person?**

A. No, this probably means that your child has a secure first attachment with you which has enabled them to build a close bond with their key person and a secure base from which to explore and learn in the setting.

Q. **How does attachment affect a child's learning?**

A. The quality of a child's learning and the development of resilience can depend on the quality of their relationships both with their key person and with you. The importance of a secure, sensitive, responsive and consistent relationship cannot be emphasised enough.

2

An environment for learning

> **This chapter includes:**
>
> - an overview of young children learning;
> - supporting the characteristics of effective learning;
> - creating a facilitating environment;
> - further reflection: theories and trends;
> - further reading;
> - Parent file: young children learning.

Young children learning

Babies are born curious, they try out new things, become involved and generally 'have a go' without fear of failing. Young children are also constantly learning and it is the role of the adults around to ensure that they maintain their learning drive and sustain their learning on an uphill trajectory. Young children who receive positive encouragement during these early years will go on to be creative and adventurous.

Adults can support learning by providing a suitable learning environment for children, one where they can develop their resilience and curiosity. The absence of an empowering environment can encourage young children to become passive and indifferent. Young children flourish when they are able to develop through their own learning characteristics. Although children learn in a unique way, the characteristics described below are shared by all children.

It is widely recognised that the shared learning characteristics include playing and exploring, active learning, and creating and thinking critically (see Figure 2.1). Each of these areas is looked at in further detail below but in reality young children do not make distinctions in their learning. Each of the strands is intrinsically woven together and the learning that takes place is life long and ongoing.

The practitioner's role, with regard to the youngest children in their setting, is less reliant upon traditional pedagogic methods and instead focuses upon the practitioner's knowledge of child development and their commitment to building strong bonds and safe nurturing environments. The characteristics of effective learning allow practitioners to understand *how* young children learn. Once practitioners understand what children need to be able to learn, they can provide the enabling environments and the positive relationships that young children require. Once these are in place even the youngest children can then go on their own unique learning journey.

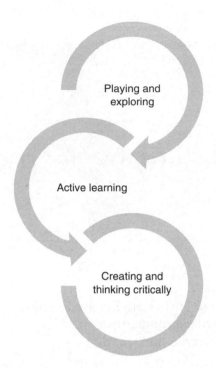

Figure 2.1   The characteristics of effective learning

Source: Based upon 'Characteristics of effective learning' in *Developing Matters in the Early Years Foundation Stage (EYFS)* 2012, p.5.

A note on schemas

Schemas are patterns of linked behaviours that are commonly observed in two year olds. Once recognised they can be used by practitioners to facilitate a child's learning.

A schema can be described as an interest in something with actions which are repeated over and over again, in an observable pattern of behaviour. Through these, babies and children can develop their awareness of the world and so deepen their learning.

Schemas develop in clusters and link together in networks, and in babies and toddlers, schemas are based in the senses and in movement. As children get older the schemas become more complex and co-ordinated as they start to 'pretend' and explore through symbolic play. All children have schemas which are influenced by their experiences and environment, people, objects and culture.

There are many kinds of schemas, some of the most common being:

- connection – joining things like train tracks or using string or ribbons;

- envelopment – covering or wrapping things up or making dens;

- trajectories – lining up objects or moving to and fro (horizontal); building towers, pouring, throwing, jumping up and down (vertical);

- transporting – carrying things or pushing prams and carts;

- scattering – spreading small objects around, stamping in puddles.

Once recognised, a schema can be tapped into in order to develop the child's learning. It also can inform planning and resourcing.

Children who have similar schemas will tend to come together and will learn from each other and will often play amicably.

Supporting the characteristics of effective learning

Providing for playing and exploring

To support young children to play and explore and develop a confident 'can do' attitude provide:

'Open-ended' resources

These encourage young children to play, explore and create. These resources do not have limits and can be used in a variety of ways by children. 'Closed resources' dictate to children what the play should be and often restricts children's flow.

'Open-ended' resources can include cardboard boxes, blocks, duplo, collections of materials, natural objects such as sticks and stones, pebbles and shells, sand, water, blankets, play dough, creative materials and dressing-up materials.

Sensory experiences will still be very important and these should be plentiful opportunities to explore a variety of materials in different ways.

Resources and equipment that reflect children's recent experiences or current interests

These could be based upon a visit or a trip a child has made, a favourite book or character or any other starting point where a child has shown curiosity.

Flexible, accommodating and safe spaces

Provide a well-managed and ordered physical environment, both indoors and outdoors, where children can play without being interrupted and where they can easily access the materials they need.

Adults need to:

Provide and plan for a continuous, ever developing provision that meets the growing learning needs of the young children in their care.

Develop playfulness and remember that the development of the characteristics of effective learning is lifelong, so enjoy the learning experiences that you share with young children.

Show children you are interested in their play and discovery and use sensitivity to join in without taking over. Show wonder if something surprises or delights you.

Consider the plan, do, review approach and focus on what children do and say rather than on what they produce as an end product.

Notice children and respect their efforts and persistence. Be mindful that children's play and exploration is their work and be careful not to appear to judge their efforts.

Providing for enthusiastic, active learners

To support young children to show persistence, enjoyment and involvement, provide:

Opportunities which encourage children's independence and choice

Two year olds are naturally curious; they want to explore and discover. Young children will attempt many things simply because they want to, and when they are encouraged to make a choice they will receive satisfaction from both choosing and from doing. This, in turn, provides the motivation to continue with the activity or the challenge and is referred to as intrinsic motivation. Intrinsically motivated children are both involved in their own learning and will remember what they have learned. Children will then go on to set their own goals for their play and activities.

Practitioners can support children by:

- encouraging children to select resources, help them to 'plan and do' and to decide what they would like to use;

- encouraging children to talk about their learning including any difficulties or problems they have come across. Try not to offer solutions immediately but ask them what they think they could do to resolve the situation.

Have safe but challenging play opportunities for children both indoor and outdoor. Plan for young children not only to take part in familiar activities but also encounter new experiences. The familiar will reassure them and provide an opportunity to consolidate skills, and the new will stimulate their learning and will extend their play. Encourage 'safe' risk-taking and new challenges. Try to pay particular attention to the youngest and quietest children.

Facilitate play and thinking by being resourceful with the materials that you offer; look to the examples of 'forest school' type activities to encourage children to become deeply involved in their play. Allow young children the time and the choice to become engrossed in activities of their own choosing without the need for clearing up and tidying away too frequently.

Adults need to:

Talk to children about their plans for their activities, try to work out if you can assist them so that they can extend or become more focused on the task they have given themselves. Encourage even the youngest children to set goals for their play and become aware of different approaches. Take a genuine interest in their play and exploration without taking over their ideas. Follow children's lead and give them the space and time to become absorbed in activities. This may mean overseeing the sharing of equipment and resources.

Praise children for their efforts as this will encourage them to increase their learning capacity but be aware that some praise can appear as judgemental or hypercritical and may take away the child's independence and confidence, for example, 'well done but are you not going to make it taller?'

Praise children for:

- trying different approaches;

- persevering;

- refusing to give up;

- solving problems;

- showing attention to detail;

- having new ideas;

- having a go.

Providing for creativity and thinking

Learning how to be creative and think critically is one of the main aspects of developing individuality. These skills are an essential aspect of being a human being and are core to young children making progress with their learning.

Young children learn most through play as it is through play that children can begin to expand on their own experience and on what they have seen and heard. The practitioner's main role in this learning area is to provide **rich play experiences** as play should be looked at in the widest sense and not just in relation to an imaginative play area, although this is a core experience. Build in time and opportunity for children to explore and handle materials, follow up on experience, and find ways to represent and explore their own ideas. In order to do this, routines may need to be flexible and resources need to be open ended and without limits.

Adults need to:

Spend time supporting children to make the sorts of connections that produce frequent 'light bulb' moments by providing them with the tools to make breakthroughs. These tools could include:

- the language of thinking and learning;

- reminding children of any previous interests or similar situations that they may have had and allow them to make the connections between experiences and opportunities;

- sharing thinking aloud with children but try to allow them to make their own associations;

- role-modelling, being a learner, showing curiosity, puzzlement and wonder;

- encouraging wider thinking by 'talking your way through' a task is one way and also by adding 'but I could also do it this way … ';

- using open-ended questions to expand thinking, for example, 'I wonder what would happen if you … ' 'what should we do next … ?' 'what else can you do with the … ' 'tell me about your … ';

- giving young children the time they need to think and do, this could be in relation to not stopping them to fit in with routines or when talking and engaging with them;

- using photographs and learning journals to encourage children to reflect and make the links between what they learned before and what they need to do now.

Promoting the characteristics of effective learning

(Use the prompts below to support your observations and planning)

Playing and exploring

- Curiosity
- Level of engagement
- Particular interests
- Taking a sensory approach
- Making a symbol out of an object, e.g. a pebble is a car
- Using own experiences in play
- Seeking new experiences
- Having a go
- Learning from previous mistakes
- Initiating play

Active learning

- Attention and focus
- Motivation
- Concentration
- Persistence
- Flexibility
- Methodology
- Enjoyment and satisfaction

Creativity and critical thinking

- Do they have their own ideas?
- Can they find ways to solve problems?
- Can they find new ways of doing things?
- Are they making links?
- Are they able to predict?
- Are they able to use skills of sequencing?
- Can they put into groups?
- Do they understand cause and effect?
- Are they planning?
- Do they strive to reach a goal?
- Are they able to change strategy?
- Can they review the process?

A note on the early development of 'learning styles'

Successful practitioners know their children well. They can tell you about the interests of the child and can recognise a child's preferred way of exploring and learning. Two year old children will use a variety of learning styles and will not yet show a distinct preference although one may be beginning to emerge. To support children to learn it is useful, however, for practitioners to have an understanding of the learning styles which may be developing. Practitioners can then ensure that varied and effective learning opportunities exist within their setting.

Kinaesthetic-tactile learners will enjoy:

- 'Moving and doing' activities, for example, outdoor play, dance and musical activities.

- Doing whatever is being talked about, for example, during a story stamp their feet.

- Moving around or 'fiddling' with something while listening or talking.

- Being demonstrative and showing physical excitement such as 'talking' with their hands.

- Touching things in order to learn about them sometimes enthusiasm may lead to snatching and grabbing!

It is likely that most two year olds will show a preference for kinaesthetic learning.

Auditory learners will enjoy:

- Talking and hearing explanations, they may like to express themselves.

- Talking out loud and repeating what they have heard.

- Having things explained, for example, enjoy listening to adults.

- Talking to themselves while learning something new.

- Repeating new things they have learned, for example, repeats what the practitioner says during activities.

Visual learners will enjoy:

- Remembering visual details and will enjoy stories with props or pictures.

- Seeing what they are talking about and enjoys seeing things work, for example, watching worms, filling and pouring water.

(Continued)

- Responding to the use of visual timetables and photographs.

Use the insight you have gained to support and plan for a child's needs by incorporating interests and learning styles into all your planning for learning.

Creating a facilitating environment

When creating an appropriate learning environment for two year olds practitioners have many things to consider, such as the smooth running of their early years setting and meeting the physical and care needs of young children, whilst considering how young children learn and develop.

The physical environment

For many two year olds an early years setting can be an overwhelming, noisy and busy environment. A warm nurturing home from home type of atmosphere is more suited to the needs of most two year olds. A predictable but stimulating environment with plenty of opportunities for sensory experiences and exploration will provide both security and a base from which children can explore and learn.

- Appraise your setting by getting down to a child's level and seeing it as they do.

- Provide child-sized places for 'one-on-one moments' between children and children and children and adults.

- Have some vertical surfaces for painting and drawing at a child's level.

- Have plenty of space for working on the floor, have carpeted areas or use builders' trays.

- Limit furniture such as tables and chairs.

- Provide soft furnishings such as sofas for stories and cuddles.

- Make sure sand and water trays are of a suitable height or are floor based.

- Use natural and heuristic type materials whenever possible to allow for continued sensory exploration.

- Have designated areas outside or inside and particular spaces where running about is encouraged.

- Have small and cosy play areas.

- Set up some areas that are shielded from pathways, exits and so on. This stops 'walk through' which also often leads to knock over!

- Have a quiet area where children can go to relax, calm down or just be by themselves for a while. This can be an area with a low screen around it or even be a tent or den to feel safe and secure inside.

- Make sure that each child has a small piece of personal space to store their belongings

Planning for activities and resources

- Make sure there are resources and materials to allow different children to access the same activity at their own unique level.

- Anticipate and plan for the children who may need support at different activities either to help them access an activity or to extend the activity.

- Ensure that there are sufficient resources to allow children to share effectively or take turns but not an over-abundance of materials taking up all available space.

- Set up activities in a way that minimises overcrowding. Have clear ways of showing when an area is 'full' or how many children should be at an activity.

- Provide resources that will encourage collaborative play and that will enhance any interest in a schema.

- Make sure that you have thought about and planned for children with a variety of needs and learning styles.

The effective and flexible use of routines

- Have established routines but with some flexibility built in, these provide a sense of safety and reassurance for most young children.

- Have an element of predictability so that children know what is happening and what to expect from each session.

- Make sure that you talk about and prepare children for changes in the routine such as special visitors, trips or new activities.

- Give advance warning when an activity is about to change or stop.

- Allow for those children who may want to continue later by helping them to put away their, for example, model or painting in a safe place so that they can return to it.

- Establish manageable turn-taking systems for activities or toys which are in high demand, such as bikes!

- Be prepared to 'go with the flow'.

Photo 2.1 Outside with sand and containers

Further reflection: theories and trends	
Cognitive constructivism A theory about the emergence and development of children's thinking. The child is actively engaged in learning with a focus on self-initiated discovery. Cognitive development follows universal and invariant stages. The idea and term 'schema' is linked to Piaget.	J. Piaget
Social constructivism A child's cognitive development is a social process within a social matrix. Learning based on real-life experiential learning. Focus on the teacher as facilitator and the idea of the 'zone of proximal development'.	L. Vygotsky
Discovery learning/Constructivism This stresses the importance of learning through discovery and problem-solving. Idea of adults 'scaffolding' children's learning to support, challenge and extend understanding. The importance of culture and language in developing thinking and constructing understanding.	J. Bruner
An individualised approach to teaching and learning which sees teachers and parents take on the role of children's learning partners, as facilitators and co-constructors of learning. The environment is the third teacher as children are agents of their own learning.	Reggio Emilia
A system of early childhood education which has four components, the curriculum, assessment tools and practitioner's methods and training. An emphasis on well-being, active learning and the plan-do-review cycle.	Highscope

Figure 2.2

Further reading

Athey, C. (2003) *Extending Thought in Young Children: A Parent-Teacher Partnership.* London: Paul Chapman.

Bruce, T. (2011) *Early Childhood Education.* 4th revd edn. London: Hodder Education.

Call, N. and Featherstone, S. (2011) *The Thinking Child: Brain-based Learning for the Early Years Foundation Stage.* 2nd edn. London: Continuum.

Clare, A. (2012) *Creating a Learning Environment for Babies and Toddlers.* London: SAGE.

Gascoyne, S. (2012) *Treasure Baskets & Beyond: Realizing the Potential of Sensory-rich Play.* Maidenhead: Open University Press.

Gray, C. and MacBlain, S. (2012) *Learning Theories in Childhood.* London: SAGE.

Harms, T., Cryer, D. and Clifford, R.M. (2006) *Infant/Toddler Environment Rating Scale.* New York: Teachers College Press.

Hodgman, L. (2011) *Enabling Environments in the Early Years: Making Provision for High Quality and Challenging Experiences in Early Years Settings.* London: Practical Pre-school Books.

McTavish, A. (2013) *Playing and Exploring (Learning and Teaching in the Early Years).* London: Practical Pre-School Books.

Nutbrown, C. (2006) *Threads of Thinking: Young Children Learning and the Role of Early Education.* London: SAGE.

Stewart, N. (2011) *How Children Learn: The Characteristics of Effective Learning.* London: British Association for Early Childhood Education.

Wood, E. (2013) *Play, Learning and the Early Childhood Curriculum.* 3rd edn. London: SAGE.

Parent file

Young children learning

How young children learn

Babies are born with a natural curiosity and children and adults are constantly learning as learning is lifelong. Young children in particular learn by playing and exploring and learn best when they are given the space and time to become involved, have the opportunity to 'have a go' and when they are encouraged to think and share their ideas.

You can help your child to learn by:

- Thoughtfully joining in their play and allowing them to take the lead.

- Encouraging them to explore by introducing them to **open-ended** activities, i.e. activities that can go on and develop in the way they choose such as building bricks, playing with sand and water, play dough or through pretend play.

- Giving them opportunities for uninterrupted time to play and explore.

- Allowing them to stop and look when they are outdoors. Young children love take their time and look at or touch all manner of things from watching a bird to splashing in a puddle.

- Encouraging them to try out new toys, books and activities – but remember they will always like to go back to 'old favourites'.

- Offering your child a running commentary on what you are doing especially when you are carrying out chores at home e.g. 'now I am going to lay the table…'.

- Model the language of learning when you are playing alongside your child say things such as 'I think…' 'How else can I do this'; 'I'm try to'; 'I wonder what will happen if I…'.

- Allow your child free access to their toys and books as this will allow them to make choices about their play and become more independent.

- Notice what your child becomes curious about and try to help them to broaden their play, e.g. if your child loves water play let them wash the dishes with you and use water and a paint brush or cloth to 'clean' their toys or the garden furniture, etc.

- If your child loves a book such as *Dear Zoo* try to extend their interest by playing with small world animal toys with them or by having a trip to a real zoo.

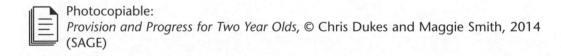

Communication and language development

> **This chapter includes:**
>
> - an overview of communication and language development 16–36 months;
> - appropriate expectations;
> - focus on practice;
> - further reflection: theories and trends;
> - further reading;
> - Parent file: making the most of one-on-one moments.

An overview

Communication and language lie at the heart of young children's development and lay the foundations for much of their future learning. It is inextricably linked with children's social and emotional development, making friends and sharing in group activities, and also in learning how to behave. So much depends also on being able to understand as well as to be understood in order to access play and wider learning opportunities which form the basis for later literacy and other skills.

This age is seen as a window of opportunity, a time between infancy and early childhood when some toddlers experience 'vocabulary spurts' when vocabulary expands rapidly. The young child's curiosity seems insatiable as they continually talk and babble to themselves and ask the names of objects to anyone around. They then repeat the named object to themselves, sometimes over and over again. At this stage a child may have a range of words or sounds from 50 to 500 words. Those at the youngest end of this developmental stage may just be beginning to be understood by those outside their immediate circle of family and friends. Children at the upper end of this developmental stage will be able to be understood by those who are not so familiar with them. There may still be mispronunciations and immature language quirks. Their own needs are very important to them and they often make them known to others by shouting, pointing or using simple words. As young children move towards the later months of this age and stage, their developing language and communication skills are trying to keep pace with the contents of their own imagination.

One of the greatest pleasures for both practitioners and parents, however, is watching a child's sense of self beginning to develop, as youngsters begin to define themselves as separate people who want to do things for themselves. Young children begin to have their own ideas about how things should happen, especially in relation to their care, begin to express what they like or dislike and what they want and do not want to do. They are often very vocal and noisy in putting their point of view forward and practitioners and parents begin to hear the word 'no' many times each day. As young children struggle towards independence, they begin to explore their environment and experience a wide variety of emotions, such as satisfaction and joy as well as anger. This is sometimes called the 'terrible twos' but it is important to remember that children are understanding much more than they are able to express and any resulting behaviours are often caused by the frustration of not being able to explain themselves clearly to those around them.

The relentless pace of language and communications development will be stimulated by the opportunities offered to children both at home and across the curriculum within the early years setting. Practitioners have the chance to turn every moment of the day into a learning experience. Children should be encouraged to talk, talk, talk, as at this age practice really does make perfect. Practitioners become the audience for children, and their active and friendly listening provides children with the validation and recognition they need to think of themselves as effective communicators.

It should be remembered, however, that each child arriving at an early years setting will be unique; some will be well on the way to developing excellent communication and language skills, while others may have had limited stimulation or language experiences. It is also important to remember that children develop at different times and in different ways, development will not necessarily be sequential and that their rate of progress in some areas may be faster than in others.

Generally, children who are having difficulties and who may need support become obvious to those who work closely with them. However, needs may vary; some might have difficulties in the articulation of words but may have well-developed understanding, expression or social interaction. Often concerns are interconnected; for example, children who have difficulties in expressing themselves may find social interactions quite a challenge. Sometimes these children will only need extra time and patience; others may require extra input and support from parents, practitioners and, perhaps, a speech and language therapist.

The diagrams in this chapter outline appropriate expectations for the age range 16–36 months. However, it is important to remember that young children develop at different rates and should be looked at individually and holistically.

16–26 months

Appropriate expectations – Receptive language/understanding

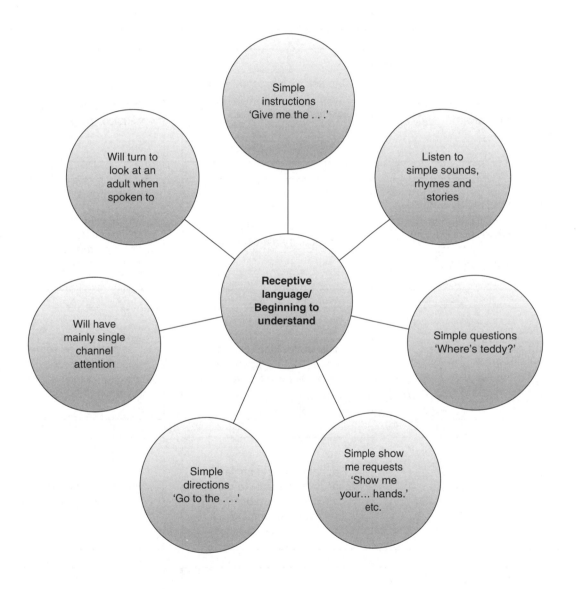

16–26 months

Appropriate expectations – Expressive language/speaking

Tries to use words that may not yet be clear

Mutters and talks to self when engaged in activity

Can say 'no' and beginning to show possession, e.g. 'mine'

Spontaneously uses up between 50 and 200 words (or more)

Can ask for what they want using words or gestures pointing saying 'uhuh' or 'mama'

Asks for specific things by name, e.g. 'milk' or 'juice', 'biscuit' etc.

Puts simple words and gestures together, e.g. 'whatssat' while pointing, 'me me' when talking with outstretched arms

Adds new words to vocabulary almost daily

Hands over and names familiar objects and toys on request

Can copy and produce animal sounds, e.g. 'moo' for cow

Begins to combine two words into meaningful phrases such as 'Bye bye mama'

Begins to use some describing words such as 'big', 'cold', 'hungry'

Begins to ask simple questions, e.g. Where Daddy? 'Home now?'

Repeats adults (echolalia) especially the last word in a sentence before absorbing into their own vocabulary

Enjoys singing and will attempt to join in

Uses telegraphic speech such as 'Mummy car', which could have several meanings

Begins to listen with some interest to general talk

Says some two-word sentences such as 'more juice' or 'all gone'

Signposts for further action 16–26 Months

These points may prompt you to carry out more detailed observations, discussion, action planning and monitoring of progress:

- a child using more gestures than words;
- not putting or beginning to put two words together;
- not wanting to join other children's play;
- does not understand words for everyday objects;
- does not imitate everyday actions;
- unable to concentrate for very short periods on activities they have chosen.

A note about soothers (dummies)

Toddlers may arrive at pre-school and still be using a soother or dummy, which can contribute to delayed communication and language development. Babies and toddlers practise the skills they need for talking by making noises and babbles using their mouth and voice. Babbling also encourages adults and other children to interact with them in the beginnings of conversation. Dummies cause babies and toddlers to make fewer sounds and so communicate less with those around them. They also prevent toddlers making normal movements at the front of their mouth. Continued sucking of a dummy and talking with it in their mouth can even lead to toddlers developing distorted patterns of speech which can be difficult to change later on. Parents need to be encouraged to limit the use of dummies for particular times, such as when a child is upset and needs comfort or as part of a sleep routine.

22–36 months

Appropriate expectations – Receptive language/understanding

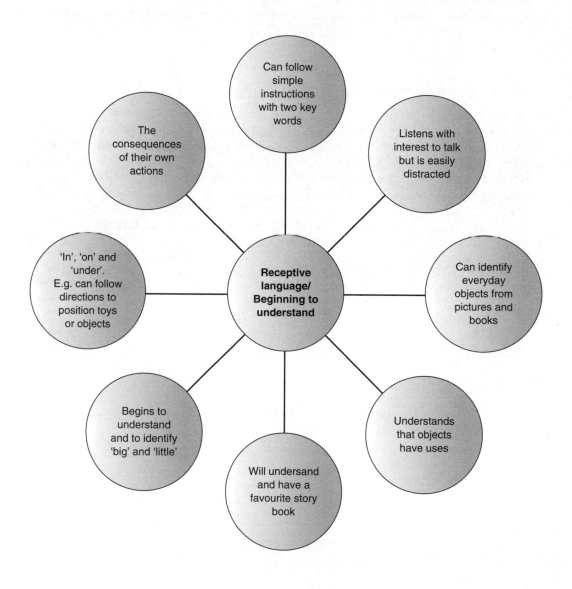

Receptive language/Beginning to understand

- Can follow simple instructions with two key words
- The consequences of their own actions
- Listens with interest to talk but is easily distracted
- 'In', 'on' and 'under'. E.g. can follow directions to position toys or objects
- Can identify everyday objects from pictures and books
- Begins to understand and to identify 'big' and 'little'
- Will undersand and have a favourite story book
- Understands that objects have uses

22–36 months

Appropriate expectations – expressive language/speaking

Uses up to 300 words

Asks lots of questions!

Begins to talk about past events

Uses plurals, e.g. 'toys', 'babies'

Can take two or three turns in a conversation

Can answer simple who, what or where questions, like 'What do we use to comb our hair?'

Uses 'my', 'mine, 'you' and 'me'

Joins in with some familiar songs and rhymes

Uses negatives in phrases such as 'Not go' or 'No want'

Will comment to other children during play

Can use simple sentences

Will initiate speaking to adults about everyday things

Can combine 4–5 words together

Starts to use the past tense such as stopped, pushed but can over-generalise its use. E.g. 'drinked' instead of 'drank'

Sometimes stammers when trying to think of what to say

Has difficulties with some speech sounds l, r, w, y, f, th, s, sh, ch, d, z, j

Beginning to express emotions in words and actions

Refers to him or herself by name

Signposts for further action 22–36 Months

These points may prompt you to carry out more detailed observations, discussion, action planning and monitoring of progress:

- withdrawn or quiet on a consistent basis;
- difficulty following simple instructions;
- no interest in playing with others, even adults;
- unable to concentrate for more than a few seconds;
- uses only single- or two-word phrases;
- frustration when trying to talk;
- speech which is difficult for familiar adults to understand;
- stammering.

A note about stammering or stuttering

It is not unusual for a child from about the age of 2 years and 6 months until 5 years old to go through periods when they stammer, stutter, hesitate or repeat sounds, words and phrases in their speech. Often this is at the beginning of sentences or as they take part in conversations or answer questions. This developmental non-fluency is all part of children's developing communication skills and generally should not cause undue concern. Additional advice should be sought from a speech and language therapist if the dysfluency starts to affect the child's confidence to take part in conversations, becomes a source of upset or frustration or persists for longer than three months.

Focus on practice

Ten key strategies for developing communication and language

Modelling

This means saying or repeating the word or phrase that a child wants or needs. In doing so you are 'modelling' the correct version and any new vocabulary. At this age/stage practitioners can begin to model a wider range of language and begin to introduce the use of verbs and adjectives. This can be done by building on the child's existing vocabulary. Extend one word to two or three such as 'cup' to 'small cup', 'dog' to 'jumpy dog'. This is also a good time to introduce more complex and longer words with two or three syllables. Expect some immaturities in children's pronunciation and try to offer the correct version of a word in context without drawing attention to the child's mistaken version.

Commenting or narrating

This is a key approach for enriching language and means talking about what a child is doing as they are doing it, something like a running commentary or narration. This allows the child to hear vocabulary and language in the context of a real situation. By describing what the child or the adult is doing it can help build connections between words in different situations. Sweeping the floor, for example, can bring lots of associated words, such as dirty, brush, as well as sweep. A child's attention is still very much single channelled and they are more likely to learn words that are based upon activities and things that they like and choose to do. Try to find words that directly relate to the activity that children have chosen or are engaged in.

Expanding or extending

This is as it suggests, taking something that a child has said and expanding upon it. Many children have what is sometimes referred to as telegraphic speech where speech is limited to perhaps two key words. The adult's role is then to expand upon these words to make a simple sentence, so encouraging the child to do the same. For example 'Polly bed' would be expanded to 'Polly is going to bed'. Later, when children act out and recall in more detail events from their own experience, adults can help to reinforce the sequence of these events by extending and expanding on what children say or describe. This will also aid memory as well as continuing to build on existing vocabulary.

Repeating back

A child at this stage will try to copy new words they hear or things which are said to them. (Beware as this can include inappropriate words!) It is generally common, too, at this age/stage for children to comment themselves on what they are doing as they play. Repeating back to a child allows you to check that you have understood what they have said and to make any necessary corrections without drawing attention to them. It also gives the child the satisfaction of hearing their own language acknowledged and gives positive reinforcement when they have used the word correctly. This will encourage them to use it again.

Asking open questions

Generally, questioning is best kept to minimum. When questions are used they should be as open as possible, which is harder than you think! Open-ended questions are those which have many possible answers rather than one-word or yes or no answers. As children become more confident in asking and answering questions, conversation can be stimulated and sustained by adults asking open questions. They can lead to very interesting conversations with young children.

Playing with words

This means singing songs and saying rhymes but also using spontaneous opportunities to play with words. Action songs and rhymes which children can join in with are very important and popular action songs such as 'Heads, shoulders, knees and toes' or 'The wheels on the bus' are the beginning of encouraging children to follow simple instructions. Visual props can be used to support many songs and rhymes and often add to the experience. Children also love sounds that they can create themselves or copy. Many books contain choruses or parts to join in with, like animal noises or set phrases, which children enjoy. Playing with words can continue as children enjoy alliteration and the onomatopoeia found in simple tongue-twisters and poems even if they do not fully understand every word.

Turn-taking and waiting time

A pause indicates that you may be waiting for a response and helps to establish the idea of turn taking which is essential in developing conversation and social skills. Try not to rush in when a child hesitates – rather use the three-second rule. When asking a question or seeking a response from a child – wait for at least three seconds before speaking again yourself. Adults need to be very aware of giving children the time to think and compose what they want to say and not fill every silence themselves. Any spontaneous opportunities for children to talk and take turns with other children as well as adults need to be taken advantage of. This can be done naturally through any nursery activity; the adult role at this stage is to facilitate children's growing communications with each other.

Using verbal prompts and giving choices

If a child is finding it hard to remember a word or phrase, you can prompt them with the first sound of the word or the first couple of words of a phrase. This is often enough to jog their memory and give a sense of achievement as it allows them to complete the word or phrase themselves. Alternatively you can give the child two choices which are modelled to them: 'Would you like milk or juice?' In this way they do not have to think of the word as well as say it.

Using visual prompts and gestures

Introduce exaggerated movement and mime into storytelling and occasionally issue some non-verbal instructions. Much of this comes naturally – we often point, pull faces or gesture to enhance or emphasise what we say. Body language also plays a part in conveying meaning and in using this you can support children's understanding.

Adjusting your language

Using simple, less complex sentences is another way to ensure that you are understood and models clear language for the child. Instructions are still best kept simple and it is important to gain the child's attention before starting to speak. Then short familiar sentences with emphasis on the key word(s) such as '*Show* me the *car*' or '*Give* me the *car*' can be used.

Photo 3.1   Having a chat about a new discovery

Ideas to introduce or consolidate

What's that for?

Children of this age need to begin to hear more than the symbolic names of objects, for example, more than an object name, but a brief description of the function of the object. Practitioners can help children develop this skill through role modelling, for example, 'yes a brush – for brushing my hair'. If children see and hear practitioners use this skill they will attempt to copy and develop their own descriptive language.

Looking and saying

Encourage children to increase vocabulary and begin to become aware of the world around them by modelling observational skills. Develop the habit when you are with the children of looking and saying or looking and pointing, so encouraging joint attention, for example, when outside with children say 'look quickly a cat'. Get down to the child's level and accompany your vocalisation with gesture and pointing. Children will soon catch on to this skill and may begin pointing and pulling you when they see something interesting.

Getting to know each other

Relationships often begin to change as a child's personality and language skills develop. Both practitioners and children begin to question each other and find out more about each other's needs, likes and dislikes. Children will begin to express opinions about what they do and do not like or want, and practitioners need to begin asking questions such as 'Which one would you like?' and 'What shall we do now?'. Practitioners who work with children of this age sometimes feel that this is the age when a real bond develops between practitioners and children; purposeful interactions are often a mark of this closeness.

Opportunities to share

Children are often very excited about showing their own toys, photographs, books and other things from home to others. With two year olds this activity needs to be kept informal and short, perhaps involving just walking around the setting showing their friends. By providing opportunities and support to do this, practitioners are showing children that they value them and are interested in what they have to show and say.

Learning and doing new things

Children learn new vocabulary from new experiences. Begin to prepare children for getting the most out of new experiences by encouraging *anticipation* and *prediction*. If going swimming, set up an interactive display with the children of all the types of things you need to take when visiting a swimming pool.

'Think aloud' when around the children by asking them open questions such as 'I wonder if the water will be warm at the swimming pool? 'Express your own ideas and thoughts, such as 'I'm going to have a shower before I get into the pool'.

Helping and doing

Children of this age want to please the adults around them. Expand language comprehension skills by asking children to do small chores for you, for example, '*Ask* Mary for the *pen* please'. As children grow, their confidence, understanding and memory increase and so practitioners can begin to expand the numbers of key words in instructions, for example, 'Go and *ask* Mary for the *red pen* please'.

Play instructional games

Play instructional games with the children both indoors and outdoors, such as simple stop and start games and marching games with instructions. Make them fun and not too serious, and those children who do not yet fully comprehend will be able to follow the lead of their peers. Expand these activities to begin to introduce prepositions such as 'over', 'under', 'in' and 'out'. Consolidate these skills by demonstrating actions at story times, for example, with a teddy or doll.

Listening and enjoying

Listening and attention skills are crucial in the development of good communication. By playing and talking with children in *small groups* or on a *one–to-one basis* we show them that good communication is made up of two parts: being able to express yourself and listening to others. This can also provide a safe environment for children to begin to try out and experiment with newly acquired vocabulary and other language skills.

Children with English as an additional language

Being bilingual or learning an additional or second language should in no way be viewed as a disadvantage. A child's home language is important not only for many social and cultural reasons but bilingualism can benefit children's overall academic and intellectual development and progress, with consistent and adequate input in both languages being most beneficial.

Children at this age are also usually in the early stages of learning their home language and may arrive at your setting with no previous knowledge of English. When their home language is developing securely then learning English will follow, although it may be delayed. A good starting point, therefore, is to work alongside parents to establish the child's development in their home language in order to make sure that there are no underlying speech and language difficulties.

Every child's situation will be different, as will their needs; however, the quality of their experience will depend on the quality of the relationship and interaction with significant adults and peers in both languages. It can be a frightening and over-whelming experience for a young child arriving in an environment where they are not able to understand what anyone says and where they are not able to be under-stood. Feelings of confusion and frustration can be common, but so too is the desire to communicate which will be the motivation for learning a new language.

Practitioners should be confident that by creating language-rich environments and by using strategies such as those outlined they will be supporting the language development of all children especially those who are learning English as a second or additional language.

Further reflection: theories and trends	
Communication-friendly spaces approach This focuses on the role of the environment in supporting speaking and listening skills, emotional well-being and general engagement.	Elizabeth Jarman
A storytelling curriculum This develops speaking and listening skills and is based on the idea that story making and fantasy play are the original learning tools that children use to understand and make sense of the world.	Vivian Gussin Paley
Kodàly method of music education This has been shown to impact on learning across the curriculum but particularly language development and memory.	Kodàly
Augmentative communication Makaton and Signalong are language programmes that use signs and symbols to encourage communication.	Makaton and Signalong

Figure 3.1

Further reading

Cross, K. (2007) *Introducing English as an Additional Language to Young Children: A Practical Handbook*. London: SAGE.

Department for Children, Schools and Families (DCSF) (2007) *Supporting Children Learning English as an Additional Language: Guidance for Practitioners in the Early Years Foundation Stage*. London: DCSF.

Department for Children, Schools and Families (DCSF) (2008) *Every Child A Talker: Guidance for Early Language Needs Practitioners*. London: DCSF.

Dukes, C. and Smith, M. (2007) *Developing Pre-school Communication and Language: Hands on Guides Series*. London: Paul Chapman.

Jarman, E. (2013) *Place to Talk for Two Year Olds*. London: Featherstone Education.

Miller, L. and Pound, L. (2011) *Theories and Approaches to Learning in the Early Years*. London: SAGE.

Whitehead, M. (2009) *Supporting Language and Literacy Development in the Early Years*. 2nd edn. Maidenhead: Open University Press.

Recommended websites

www.ican.org.uk

Advice and resources for practitioners and parents.

www.talkingpoint.org.uk

Useful information for parents of under threes.

www.talktoyourbaby.org.uk

Useful information for parents of under threes.

www.literacytrust.org.uk

Excellent resources to support parents.

www.elizabethjarmantraining.co.uk

www.makaton.co.uk

www.signalong.org.uk

Parent file

Making the most of one-on-one moments

Make the most of one-on-one moments with your child. These suggestions can be incorporated into those everyday tasks and activities that you share with your child such as during their personal care or at bedtime.

- Make good eye contact during care routines and when your child talks to you give them your full attention. This will encourage them to communicate more.

- When your child starts to say words, use the word to start a conversation by replying with a simple sentence, e.g. 'Mama' 'Yes I'm your Mama'.

- During care routines give a running commentary on what you are doing, leave gaps for your child to fill in missing words, e.g. 'Let's wash those. . .'

- Carry out simple tasks together, like setting the table or putting the washing away by giving simple instructions and take the opportunity to introduce new words.

- Make jokes out of activities such as dressing, say 'Is this yours?' 'Does it go on your head?' Leave time for the child to respond.

- Get into the habit of outlining the day's events and activities; ask the child's opinion on what they would like to do.

- Play simple turn-taking games together such as inset puzzles, building brick towers, playing instruments. Introduce the language of sharing, e.g. 'my turn, your turn. . .'

- Focus on the here and now and do not focus too much on the future or past, as two year olds find the concept of time difficult to grasp.

- Read picture books together; take turns telling or retelling the stories. Use family photographs to talk about individuals.

- If your child has a favourite book or story, let their key person know so that they can share it at the setting as well.

- Say or sing nursery rhymes and songs with your child that they are learning at their setting; this helps to consolidate their learning and shows your shared interest.

- Use gestures and facial expressions to reinforce new words and their meaning; if the setting uses signing such as Makaton or Signalong, try to learn some too.

- Point out familiar as well as new objects or people when you are out and about ,giving your child time to practice new words and also hear familiar ones in different contexts.

4

Physical development

This chapter includes:

- an overview of physical development 16–36 months;
- appropriate expectations;
- focus on practice;
- further reflection: theories and trends;
- further reading;
- Parent file: physical activity in everyday routines.

An overview

In the first five years of life babies and young children undergo huge changes both physically and psychologically. While babies are born with some instinctive reflexes, such as sucking, after birth, all other physical movements are learned.

This is the time to lay the foundations for future well-being and health, and good habits established in the early years last into later childhood and adulthood. The role of parents, carers and practitioners is crucial in providing babies and toddlers with the opportunities to improve their physical skills as well as develop healthy choices in relation to food, rest, sleep and exercise.

Physical activity gives children an awareness of their senses and teaches them about their bodies and the world around them. Early childhood is a window of opportunity in which to develop fundamental motor skills which do not naturally emerge but instead need to be taught and practised. Physical activity develops these essential motor skills as well as helping young children to maintain a healthy weight and build strong bones and muscles including the heart and lungs. Movement skills tend to develop in a progressive order but they are not always *determined* by the child's age and it is important to remember that there are differences in how and when individual children develop.

In addition to acquiring the physical skills, 'physical literacy' is based on developing a child's enjoyment of being active as well as offering understanding of why physical activity is important. This promotes health and well-being by fostering a positive

Areas of development which can be supported by physical activity

Stimulating important brain connections	Gross and fine motor skills	Rhythm and timing	Spatial awareness
Balance and control	Posture	Mobility	Strength
Stamina	Agility	Core, shoulder, and hand stability	Co-ordinated movement
Developing language and vocabulary	Having fun	Concentration	Feeling well and full of energy
Listening	Interacting with others	Speaking in a familiar group	Responding to questions or instructions
Taking turns	Sharing	Becoming familiar with 'rules'	Problem-solving
Decision-making	Independence	Memory skills	Making choices
Imagination and creativity	Confidence	Self-esteem	Resilience
Co-operation and collaboration	Developing empathy	Set and respond to challenge	Assessing and taking risks

attitude and will go a long way to developing a lifelong pleasure in exercise and physical activity. Most importantly too, movement and sensory activities and experiences develop important brain structures by helping to activate and organise reflexes, establishing and reinforcing connections within the brain. These connections are critical for developing vision, language and communication, social, cognitive and motor skills.

Physical activity and movement can also have far wider benefits. Physical interactive play can be important for long-term emotional health as it has natural anti-stress effects, promotes positive emotions, such as joy, and enhances the functions in the frontal lobe which regulates emotions. This lays the foundation for helping children to manage their feelings, develop resilience and build self-esteem. Conversely children who do not have enough access to this kind of play often then engage in boisterous activity at inappropriate times or find it hard to sit still or focus.

The interactions with adults and peers, which are involved in physical activities, also develop language and communication skills such as listening and attention and build vocabulary as well as opportunities to be creative and use imagination. Co-operative physical activities encourage turn-taking, sharing and getting along with others which is so crucial at this stage. It sees the beginnings of being able to understand rules for games, a sense of fairness and boundaries for behaviour.

Many physical activities also involve problem-solving and decision-making skills. This can build positive attitudes to challenge, the confidence to try new things and independence, as well as being able to ask for help when it is needed. All of these contribute to later ability to cope and adapt to stressful and changing situations. It also provides valuable first experiences in assessing and taking risks within a supportive and safe environment.

Gross motor skills

Gross motor skills are those which use whole-body movements involving posture, larger movements and the large muscles of the body. They first develop with physical co-ordination and control, beginning at a child's head, working downwards through the arms, hands and, finally, the legs and feet. Outdoor activities in particular are well suited to developing gross motor skills and most early year's settings have an outside area or access to a park or open space. Practitioners also need to give some thought to the opportunities they offer for physical activity indoors. Toddlers and young children need to be given plenty of floor space so that they can, for example, spend time on their tummy, crawling and practising some of those earlier skills.

A variety of activities and opportunities need to be offered which will develop co-ordination, strength and stamina. Particular focus can be given to developing core strength or trunk stability, which is essential for helping to maintain balance and posture when we are sitting, standing or moving. Activities include walking, running, hopping, skipping, jumping and balancing and riding bikes. Other activities to develop shoulder stability and arm and wrist strength, which later helps with hand control and accuracy, include pulling, pushing, throwing, hanging and swinging or playing with parachutes. With encouragement toddlers and young children will begin to develop object control skills such as throwing, catching, rolling or kicking a ball.

Generally most of what is needed to provide children with these opportunities can be available in early year's settings when practitioners acknowledge the wider value of these activities. The British Heart Foundation recommends 180 minutes or three hours of physical activity per day for 2–3 year olds who are able to walk, citing that the amount rather than the intensity of the physical activity is most important. Fortunately most 2–3 year olds have more than enough energy to meet this target given the right opportunities! Toddlers and young children tend to have bursts of energy followed by slightly quieter times so everyday movements such as walking or just moving about, tidying up or being a 'helper' all count towards this target as well as more vigorous dancing , running and climbing. After such a busy time many 2–3 years olds will still need a rest or a sleep to recharge their batteries.

When thinking about a child's physical development it is important to have some information from parents about when they reached various milestones. Such as when they first sat up, crawled, walked and so on. Some children are more comfortable and/or confident than others with physical activity and the skills involved. This could be as a result of a lack of experience, a previous accident or injury or even an overprotective parent. Children who experience difficulties with any aspects of physical development can be enormously supported in the early years, but for those with ongoing difficulties additional advice will need to be sought from an occupational therapist or physiotherapist. These professionals often provide specific therapy programmes and strategies which can be integrated into the planning and activities of the setting. These can usually be shared with other children in the setting as well.

It should be noted too that children who have a diagnosed or recognised physical condition may be working towards a different set of criteria. In these cases practitioners should always ensure that activities are safe and suitable. This can be ensured by working in partnership with parents, therapists and any specialist teachers who may be involved with the child.

The diagrams in this chapter outline appropriate expectations for the age range 16–36 months. However it is important to remember that young children develop at different rates and should be looked at individually and holistically.

16–26 months

Appropriate expectations – gross motor skills

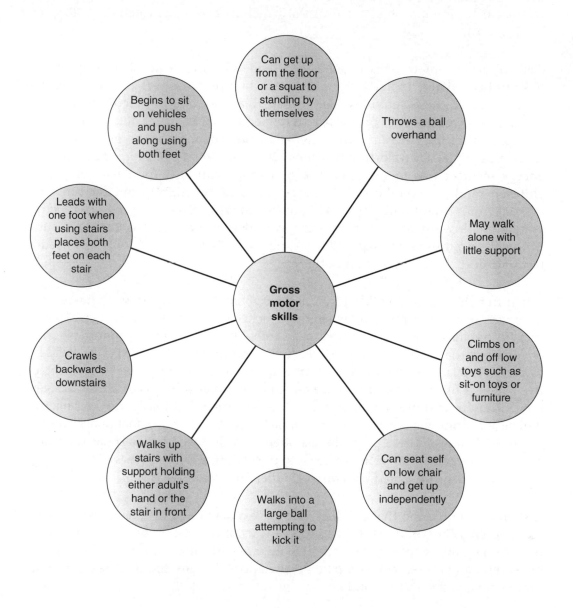

Gross motor skills

- Can get up from the floor or a squat to standing by themselves
- Throws a ball overhand
- May walk alone with little support
- Climbs on and off low toys such as sit-on toys or furniture
- Can seat self on low chair and get up independently
- Walks into a large ball attempting to kick it
- Walks up stairs with support holding either adult's hand or the stair in front
- Crawls backwards downstairs
- Leads with one foot when using stairs places both feet on each stair
- Begins to sit on vehicles and push along using both feet

22–36 months

Appropriate expectations – gross motor skills

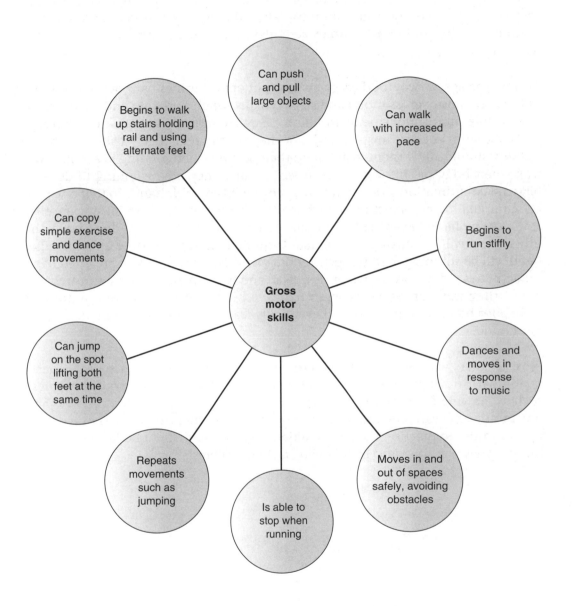

- Can push and pull large objects
- Begins to walk up stairs holding rail and using alternate feet
- Can walk with increased pace
- Can copy simple exercise and dance movements
- Begins to run stiffly
- **Gross motor skills**
- Dances and moves in response to music
- Can jump on the spot lifting both feet at the same time
- Repeats movements such as jumping
- Is able to stop when running
- Moves in and out of spaces safely, avoiding obstacles

Fine motor skills

Fine motor *skills* involve the use of the small muscles in the fingers, hand and arm in order to manipulate and control the use of tools and materials, while fine motor *control* requires awareness and planning to complete a task. It also requires muscle strength, co-ordination and normal sensation. Alongside and part of the development of these skills is the development of hand–eye co-ordination, where vision is used to control these fine motor movements. These are all important because they form the basis and foundation for later skills such as self-help and self-care, writing, drawing and more complex activities such as art, construction, music and technology.

Around the age of two, toddlers given the right opportunities have developed some of the prerequisite gross motor and sensory skills which underpin and enable more refined fine motor movements to follow. They are more aware of where different parts of their bodies are in space and how they are moving. Their balance and trunk stability should allow them to maintain their posture when rotating, reaching away from their body or shifting weight to either side. They are beginning to develop bilateral co-ordination so separating the movements of their hands so that one may be manipulating an object or tool while the other is holding or stabilising another as a 'helping hand'. Eventually, for example, one hand will be steadying a bowl, the other hand will be stirring, or one hand will be holding the paper and the other hand will be snipping with scissors. Toddlers will also start to have a preferred hand for activities. They may, however, still swap and use whichever hand is nearest the object they want or switch between hands, especially if they are getting tired or have poor hand strength. This will eventually lead to the establishment of a dominant hand.

Most toddlers will be very active and many show little interest in spontaneously taking part in the traditional types of what are labelled as 'fine motor activities', such as drawing or art and craft. This is especially true for those children who find fine motor activities difficult, who may shy away from them and so do not have the opportunities to practise. For these children practitioners can build in practice during everyday activities and by following a child's interests.

16–26 months

Appropriate expectations – fine motor skills

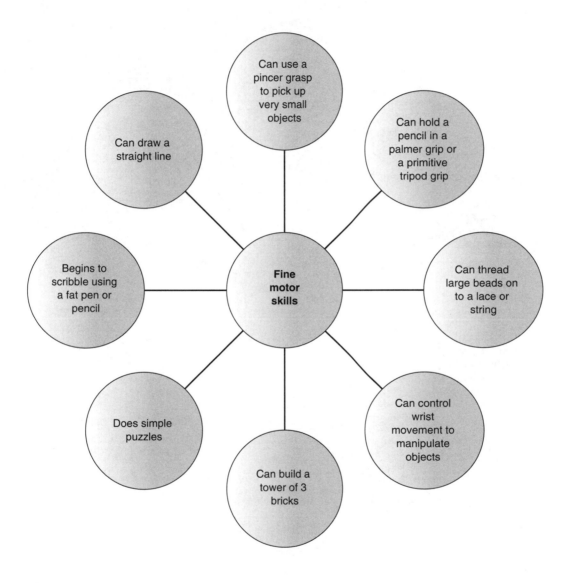

- Can use a pincer grasp to pick up very small objects
- Can hold a pencil in a palmer grip or a primitive tripod grip
- Can thread large beads on to a lace or string
- Can control wrist movement to manipulate objects
- Can build a tower of 3 bricks
- Does simple puzzles
- Begins to scribble using a fat pen or pencil
- Can draw a straight line

Fine motor skills

22–36 months

Appropriate expectations – fine motor skills

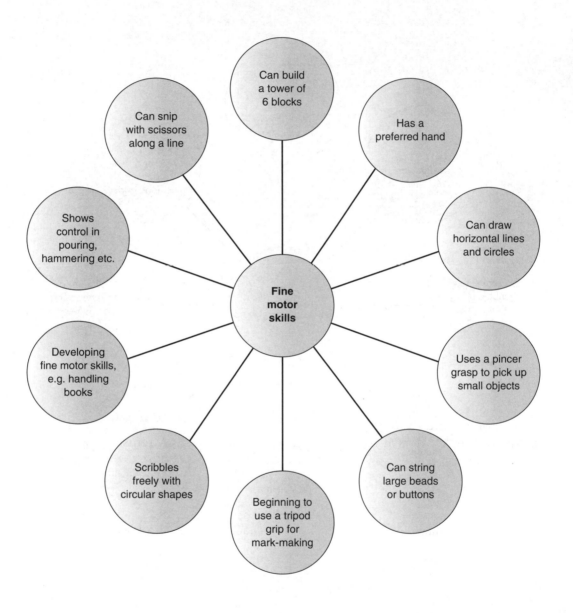

Fine motor skills

- Can build a tower of 6 blocks
- Has a preferred hand
- Can draw horizontal lines and circles
- Uses a pincer grasp to pick up small objects
- Can string large beads or buttons
- Beginning to use a tripod grip for mark-making
- Scribbles freely with circular shapes
- Developing fine motor skills, e.g. handling books
- Shows control in pouring, hammering etc.
- Can snip with scissors along a line

Self-care

This is the 'I want to do it myself' age and as children's physical skills develop they also become more independent. Children will test their limits and struggle with trying to do things for themselves while still needing help. This is often most evident in their care routines. They will also enjoy helping with everyday tasks such as preparing food or snacks, tidying or cleaning!

Dressing

Generally, toddlers are able to undress before they can dress themselves. While some will be happy to co-operate with clothes chosen for them, others often express preferences for particular colours or types of clothes or want to change several times a day, and this may be something which concerns parents in particular. A growing desire for independence means that children will want and need to be encouraged to have a go. Remember:

- As a toddler tries their hand at each new skill lots of specific praise will encourage them to try again.

- Be prepared to slow down and wait as they will need extra time and practice before they achieve success.

- Do not jump in to help too quickly, wait until they ask for help.

- Try to break down tasks so that, for example, you start doing the zipper and they finish it, in that way they experience success.

Food and eating

Many toddlers and young children develop strong likes and dislikes and can become 'faddy' or 'fussy' eaters at this age. This can manifest itself in refusing food of certain textures, a preference for a certain colour or type of food or a reluctance to try new foods. Some children will hold food in their mouth and others will immediately spit it out. It can become frustrating and distressing particularly for parents when a child has a limited diet or sometimes refuses to eat. The most important thing is not to make it an issue as this often exacerbates the problem and can turn snack or meal times into a battle. Though some children can hold out longer than others, toddlers will eat if they are hungry! It should be noted, however, that some toddlers and young children have issues with chewing or swallowing or sensory defensiveness which can be associated with other difficulties. If you are worried about any aspect then alongside parents seek advice from a health visitor or other health-care professional.

Some toddlers may arrive at your setting feeling hungry and may then not be ready to play or explore. In recognition of this, many settings now provide a breakfast table in addition to snack. Remember:

- Try to stick to a meal-time routine.

- Sit with toddlers and make eating a pleasant social activity.

- Persevere in offering small amounts of new foods even if it is not eaten at first.

- Allow children to explore food and feed themselves as much as possible as this gives them control of new experiences and allows them to try things at their own pace.

- If food is refused then indicate that it is only on offer for a limited time and then remove it.

- Try not to make food into an issue – it is never very long until the next meal time!

Toileting

Between the ages of two and three many toddlers and most young children are ready to be toilet trained, especially during the day. Those who are ready to begin training will begin to show signs of needing to go or being uncomfortable when wet or soiled. A familiar adult will learn to recognise these signs and can gently encourage and introduce a potty or the toilet. The most important thing is for practitioners and parents to work together and have a consistent, calm and patient approach. Remember:

- Ask the child regularly if they need the toilet and develop a routine which fits in with the nursery and home.

- Encourage parents to dress their child in clothes which are easy to pull down and up.

- Praise any attempts to sit on or use the potty or toilet.

- Clear up any accidents without a fuss.

- Be aware that the bathroom may hold fears for the child; many children, for example, do not like the noise of flushing or hand-driers and can become very upset.

16–26 months

Appropriate expectations – self-care

22–36 months

Appropriate expectations – self-care

- Can drink from a beaker by themselves
- Can indicate when they are wet or soiled
- Will start having some sense of danger and risk
- **Self-care**
- May be potty or toilet trained in the daytime or ready to start training
- Can feed themselves without too many spills
- Can wash and dry their hands and will attempt to clean teeth/wipe nose
- Can put on some items of clothing and starts to unzip/tries to put on shoes
- Willing to try new foods, tastes and textures

Signposts for further action

These points may prompt you to carry out more detailed observations, discussion, action planning and monitoring of progress:

16–26 months

- A toddler who has poor balance and falls over a lot from a standing position.
- A toddler who needs to be picked up or pulled onto their feet.
- A toddler not using both hands, for example steadies toy with one hand when using the other to explore an object.
- A toddler who does not get up/begin to try to move around.
- A toddler who does not begin to climb.
- A toddler who does not find a way to get up and down stairs.
- A toddler who continues to walk with a stiff gait.
- A toddler not using a pincer grasp.

22–36 months

- A young child who constantly bumps into objects both indoors and outdoors.
- A young child who is always dropping things and who has poor fine motor control.
- A young child who cannot stop safely when running.
- A young child who is lacking in confidence when undertaking physical activity.
- A young child who has trouble getting up and down the stairs.
- A young child who cannot complete simple inset puzzles (two to five pieces) with support.
- A young child who has difficulty joining in simple action songs.
- A young child who cannot throw objects.
- A young child not able to snip with scissors.
- A young child not able to self-feed with a spoon.
- Excessive mouthing of objects.

Photo 4.1   Working together to make things move

Focus on practice

Physically active play is the best way for young children to be physically active, and both indoor and outdoor active play experiences are important for a child's development.

The role of the practitioner is crucial in providing appropriate opportunities.

Introduce new and challenging skills

This is the perfect time to introduce skills which encourage stability such as riding a bike and more challenging balancing and climbing activities. Also games and equipment to promote object-control skills such as kicking, catching, throwing, striking and rolling a ball, hoop or beanbag.

Allow plenty of time for practice

As well as practising new skills children need the chance to consolidate their learning and refine their skills. Even slightly older toddlers and young children will benefit from going back over skills from earlier stages, such as:

- playing on the floor on tummies and backs;
- crawling commando style on tummies and rolling;
- crawling on all fours, such as through tunnels;
- stretching, pushing and pulling activities as these help build body awareness;
- spinning and tipping either gently or with more energy!

Create opportunities for bursts of short, highly energetic games which will leave children short of breath

Activities such as running, jumping, hopping, galloping, skipping and dancing are good and also allow children to practise their locomotor skills. Dancing, music and action songs are a great way to encourage movement and play. Rough and tumble games can be enjoyable but may need to be supervised as toddlers can easily get carried away and may end up hurting each other.

Incorporate physical activity into the routine of the nursery/home

Tidying up toys, gardening and setting up for snack and meal times all contribute to a child's physical activity.

Provide the equipment/resources

Look for a variety of open ended equipment that encourages use of large and small muscles, as well as independent activity, imagination and social contact. Large wooden blocks that can be used both indoor and outdoor are ideal.

Look for opportunities to develop fine motor skills in non-traditional activities

Almost any area of the setting can include elements of fine motor activities. Role play and home corners provide ample use for buttons, zips, pegs and cutlery, while themed areas such as shops, schools and doctors surgeries provide opportunities for pens, chalk, tongs, tweezers and scissors. Sand and play dough, cooking and construction, rhymes and finger puppets, indeed anything that will get fingers moving!

Be prepared

Practitioners need to make sure that there is plenty of room for activities and that young children are prepared for making the most of opportunities by being dressed appropriately for the activities on offer. Wellies, waterproofs, trainers, aprons, sunhats, sunscreen as well as drinking water need to be readily available.

Be a cheerleader

It is essential that practitioners encourage and support, praise achievements and successes and give positive feedback to toddlers' efforts to master these skills.

Take a back seat

As long as children are safe let them guide the games and activities, and resist the urge to interfere or hover, unless you are asked to join and play. Offer a 'helping hand' during physical exercise, such as walking along a balancing beam, but try to reduce the support to a 'helping finger' until eventually the child moves independently.

Be a role model and encourage parents to be role models too

Encourage parents to build physical activity into their everyday routines by walking or scooting to nursery, by visiting the park on the way home or at weekends, and so on.

Further reflection: theories and trends	
The importance of play in children's learning and development. Parents and family life are central to education and young children should learn in a home-like environment with outdoor as well as indoor opportunities.	Froebel
Based on an understanding that children have an innate capacity to learn and educate themselves when placed in a specifically prepared environment that allows for independence and freedom. Importance of sensory experiences and natural materials.	M. Montessori
A focus on the ability of young children to learn through imitation and activity and the world of 'house and garden'. The importance of purposeful movement indoors and outdoors which facilitates integration of sensory experiences.	Steiner Waldorf
Offers experiences in woodland settings which build confidence, emotional well-being and physicality. Also opportunities to take risks, problem-solve, explore and create. Early influences of sisters R. and M. McMillan.	The Forest School Approach

Figure 4.1

Further reading

British Heart Foundation (BHF) (2011) *National Guidelines for Physical Literacy*. London: BHF.

British Heart Foundation (BHF) (2012) *Early Movers: An Introduction to Physical Activity in the Early years*. London: BHF.

Bruce, T. (2005) *Early Childhood Education*. 3rd edn. London: Hodder and Stoughton.

Casey, T. (2007) *Environments for Outdoor Play: A Practical Guide to Making Space for Children*. London: Paul Chapman Publishing.

Department for Children, Schools and Families (DCSF) (2010) *Challenging Practice to Further Improve Learning, Playing and Interacting in the EYFS*. Crown Copyright. London: DCSF.

Knight, S. (2011) *Risk & Adventure in Early Years Outdoor Play: Learning from Forest Schools*. London: SAGE.

Knight, S. (2013) *Forest Schools and Outdoor Learning in the Early Years*. 2nd edn. London: SAGE.

Macintyre, C. (2002) *Early Intervention in Movement: Practical Activities for Early Years Settings*. London: David Fulton.

Sheridan, M., Sharma, A. and Cockerill, H. (2007) *From Birth to Five Years: Children's Developmental Progress*. 3rd edn. Oxford: Routledge.

Warden, C. and Buchan, N. (2012) *Nurture Through Nature: Working with Children Under 3 in Outdoor Environments*. 2nd revd edn. Auchterarder: Mindstretchers.

Whitehead, M. (2010) 'The concept of physical literacy', in M. Whitehead (ed.), *Physical Literacy throughout the Lifecourse*. Oxford: Routledge.

Recommended websites

www.forestschools.com
Information for parents and practitioners.

www.bhfactive.org.uk
Research-based evidence leading the way in promoting physical activity and healthy lifestyles. Resources and information for practitioners.

Parent file

Physical activity in everyday routines

Try to build physical activity into everyday routines, be a role model and most of all make it fun!

- Walk to pre-school instead of taking the buggy; try to make it fun by hopping or skipping or jumping some of the way!

- If travelling by car, park a short distance away to allow extra time for some walking.

- Get toddlers and young children moving around your home running errands for you.

- Encourage helping with everyday activities like cooking, stirring, preparing food, washing up, even sweeping the floor or washing the car.

- Children love to help to dig. They can help you or a neighbour, plant bulbs, water the garden or rake the leaves.

- Join in with action rhymes and songs and encourage dancing to your favourite pop songs.

- Encourage toddlers to spend time on their tummy or knees by playing with games or toys on the floor.

- Try to have a regular time to go to the park or playground, arrange to meet friends so children can play together.

- Take a ball, a hoop or Frisbee, or play some chasing games or races.

- Blow bubbles to chase or pop.

- Water play or swimming is an excellent way to keep moving and have fun.

5

Personal, social and emotional development

> **This chapter includes:**
>
> - an overview of personal social and emotional development 16–36;
> - appropriate expectations;
> - focus on practice;
> - further reflection: theories and trends;
> - further reading;
> - Parent file: supporting personal, social and emotional development.

An overview

Personal, social and emotional development underpins all areas of a young child's progress and learning. All children need to be supported and encouraged to develop a secure sense of self as well as to begin to develop the important skills necessary to make friends and begin to get along well with others. Creating a warm, emotional environment can be seen as the starting point for welcoming two year olds into your setting. For children, being special to someone is fundamental to their personal, social and emotional health and well-being.

From birth, babies and young children need far more than only their physical needs met. Although nourishment in the form of food and warmth is vital, it is also essential for a young child to feel safe and nurtured. Once they know that they are safe and loved they can begin to explore the world. A young child will build on these feelings of security and, although they may want to stay close to their caregivers, they will be able to relax and begin to investigate and enjoy the stimulating environment that has been provided for them. Having secure attachments and being acknowledged and affirmed by the important people in their lives will lead to children gaining confidence and inner strength. This in turn promotes a sense of belonging which further allows children to explore the world from a secure base.

Young children need the adults around them to provide them with opportunities for interaction so that they can develop positive ideas about themselves in relation to others, it is then they can move on to learn and discover, develop empathy, and ultimately live in harmony with their peers and those adults around them.

Children who feel secure in their relationships can go on to express their ideas and feelings, such as joy, sadness, excitement, wonder, frustration and fear. They begin to develop resilience and strategies to cope with new and challenging or stressful situations. Finally, they will go on to develop a positive sense of well-being.

A positive working relationship with the parents of the two year olds in your care is vital. Through active involving, connecting and communicating with parents, practitioners will get to know children better. Shared and detailed knowledge about a young child between parent and practitioner will ensure that a child is viewed holistically and that practitioners will know how best to meet an individual's needs. Some disadvantaged children may start their early learning without the advantages that feeling secure and loved bring. The least advantaged children may bring the greatest challenges for practitioners, and it is these children who will need additional time, patience, consistency and love from the caregivers around them.

Practitioners can be the most stable element in the lives of some children and this in turn brings responsibilities and raises issues around managing key working, and staff shifts, holiday cover and so on which need to be thought through and carefully balanced with the needs of the most vulnerable two years olds and their families. All early year's practitioners need to be aware that children, like adults, have a wide and varied home life and experience different relationships. They are part of a family and a wider community as well as members of the setting community. Children's personal, social and emotional development does not occur in isolation, but is dependent upon those circumstances that children find themselves in and on the significant adult relationships that they have.

That is why early years practitioners have always viewed children holistically. Children, even those who seem secure and thriving, can be affected by circumstances which are beyond their control. Practitioners should be mindful that two year olds have not yet built up enough resilience to deal with many of the circumstances they may encounter. Practitioners should be alert to any upsets or changes in a child's life and be prepared to offer them extra security and support when they need it.

Some of these factors may include:

- parent or relative away or in hospital;
- a new or different carer or childminder;
- not sleeping well or has disturbed nights;
- illness or bereavement in the family;
- parent has a new partner;
- parents separating or divorcing;
- a new baby in the family;
- living in temporary or unsatisfactory accommodation;
- living with hardship or poverty;
- domestic violence within the home;
- family are new to the country or region;
- issues around drugs or alcohol misuse;
- changes in the daily routine or absence of routines.

The diagrams in this chapter outline appropriate expectations for the age range 16–36 months. However, it is important to remember that young children develop at different rates and should be looked at individually and holistically.

16–26 months

Appropriate expectations

Personal, social and emotional development

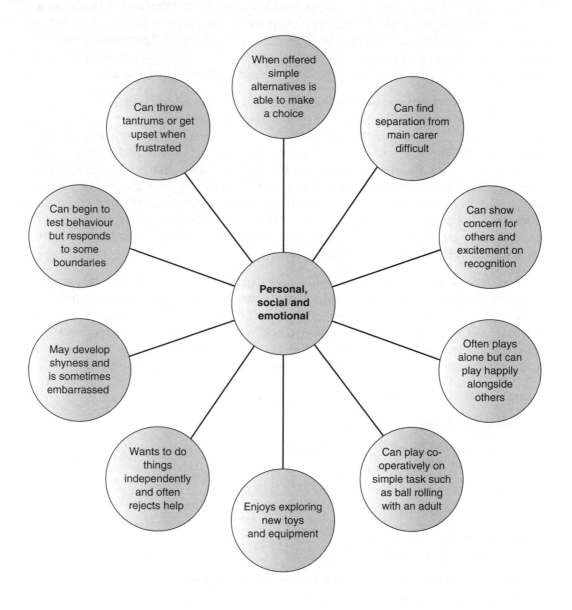

When offered simple alternatives is able to make a choice

Can throw tantrums or get upset when frustrated

Can find separation from main carer difficult

Can begin to test behaviour but responds to some boundaries

Can show concern for others and excitement on recognition

Personal, social and emotional

May develop shyness and is sometimes embarrassed

Often plays alone but can play happily alongside others

Wants to do things independently and often rejects help

Can play co-operatively on simple task such as ball rolling with an adult

Enjoys exploring new toys and equipment

22–36 months

Appropriate expectations

Personal, social and emotional development

- Likes to make choices and begins to show preferences
- Is affectionate towards 'their' special people or friends
- Separates from main carers with support
- Has favourite activities
- Aware of other children and what they are doing, may begin to play co-operatively
- Likes to help those around and responds well to praise
- Becoming aware of the feelings of others
- Is becoming more independent but may need a key person to turn to
- Can show some restraint and can stop themselves from acting spontaneously

Personal, social and emotional

Signposts for further action

These points may prompt you to carry out more detailed observations, discussion, action planning and monitoring of progress:

16–26 months

- A toddler who does not participate or try 'to help' when getting dressed and undressed.
- A toddler who shows little interest in eating and drinking.
- A toddler who demands little attention and does not engage with caregivers.
- A toddler who is unable to amuse themselves with objects or toys for a short period.
- A toddler who does not demonstrate affection with caregiver and other familiar adults and children.
- A toddler who does not try to participate or join in during singing and nursery rhymes.
- A toddler who seems detached from those around.
- A toddler who shows little curiosity or desire to explore their own environment.

22–36 months

- A young child who does not like to join in play one-on-one with a known adult.
- A young child who shows no interest in feeding or dressing themselves.
- A young child who shows no discomfort when wearing a dirty nappy/pants.
- A young child who shows little interest in their peers.
- A young child who is non-co-operative most of the time.
- A young child who shows little pride in any activity they have participated in, for example, their play dough model or painting.
- A young child who shows no desire for independence and allows adults to meet their basic needs, for example, feeding, toileting.
- A young child who does not seem to be aware of what is going on around them and shows little attention to danger.

Photo 5.1 Taking baby for a walk in the pram

 Focus on practice

Show concern and affection

Try to provide emotional consistency that is, remaining steady in your everyday dealing with children no matter what your personal feelings or emotions may be at that time. Young children have remarkable insight and they can sense when adults are unconditionally there for them. Allow yourself and other staff to develop emotional bonds.

Home sweet home

Make your setting a 'home from home' where children feel happy and comfortable. View your setting through the eyes of a two year old and consider what it looks and feels like to them. Take stock of your environment and make any changes you feel necessary to make your setting feel like a safe haven.

Be demonstrative and provide physical accessibility

Have appropriate physical contact with two year olds, hug them, sit them on your knee and hold their hand when you need to – be natural! And remember it is important to have one-on-one time as often as possible, even within a busy room.

Be playful and be a friend to children

Join in and have fun with the children by being a playmate and a supportive friend; you will almost always be guaranteed a positive response. Think about playing games such as 'roll the ball to and fro', 'this little piggy went to market', 'hand clapping games' and so on.

Trust your feelings

Be intuitive about what individual children need. Once practitioners get to know children they often become perceptive and develop a sense of the sort of things a child may need or may be feeling. Trust your instincts and be spontaneous.

Provide emotional security

Try to be adaptable when changes occur within the setting. Appear confident in front of the children and parents, especially when adjustments are made to the environment such as routines or staff change. Remember, young children will take their lead and will get their feelings of security from you.

Promote friendships

Build social bridges for those children who need them to assist them to make successful social interaction with the other children or even other staff. You can do this by asking them to give, get or say something to someone else on your behalf. If you do this often enough eventually the child will feel confident enough to make contact on their own behalf.

Be aware of children within the room

Even if you are not engaged with young children, remember to constantly check by looking, listening or making some other contact. This contact could be eye contact or a non-verbal signal such as a 'head bob' or a smile to let children know you are aware of them. Young children could be encouraged to do the same with you, this encourages children to feel secure and allows them to continue their play confidently.

Try to forget adult timescales

Give plenty of time when promoting self-help skills such as toileting, hand-washing, putting shoes on, and so on. Young children dislike being hurried and for some it can promote a sense of panic and frustration. Allow plenty of time for children to develop their own skills at their own pace.

Role-model positive relationships

Always try to model good social skills with your colleagues and especially with the child's parents/carers. Young children are often fascinated by adults' relationships and tend to copy what they see.

Offer preferences

Even the youngest children appreciate being offered preferences and alternatives. This is a simple way to affirm that the young child is regarded by staff and is trusted to make good decisions. With two year olds remember to keep the choices to a simple this or that. Think through your day and your routines, and note down all of the times when children can be asked to express a preference.

Be alert to changes in emotions

Two year olds can go from calm to cross in a matter of seconds! Be alert to a child's mood and if you can see frustration setting in use a distraction technique to diffuse a situation. Most two year olds can be distracted quite easily if the mood is caught in time.

Create a sense of ownership

Try to create a sense of community and joint ownership as this will encourage children to look after the setting and equipment. When introducing new equipment or new experiences to young children, talk to them and prepare them for using it or by guide them on how to participate. Support children's efforts to share but do not expect them to be able to do this all of the time.

Supporting children to begin to share and take turns

At the age of two it is unrealistic to expect children to be able to share and take turns before they arrive at a setting. Two year olds are generally egocentric and self-absorbed and will find sharing difficult. They will need the support, direction and patience of friendly adults to help them share space, equipment, activities and, most of all, adult time.

Further reflection: theories and trends	
Social learning theory Theory which emphasises the importance of children imitating and identifying with those around them.	A. Bandura
The part played by the wider influences in society in children's learning and development.	
Motivation and self-efficacy as central to educational development.	U. Bronfenbrenner
Laevers: an approach to experiential education which looks at the educational experience from the child's point of view. It promotes stimulating and sensitive environments and practitioners that allow for deep level learning and support children's social and emotional well-being.	F. Laevers
Leuven Child Involvement Scales: these focus on children's emotional well-being and levels of involvement.	Laevers and Moon

Figure 5.1

Further reading

Allen, G. (2011) *Early Intervention: The Next Steps*. London: HM Government.

Arnold, C. (2011) *Understanding Schemas and Emotion in Early Childhood*. London: SAGE.

Brownlee, P. (2008) *Dance With Me in the Heart*. Auckland: New Zealand Playcentre Publications.

Dowling, M. (2010) *Young Children's Personal, Social and Emotional Development*. 3rd edn. London: SAGE.

Dukes, C. and Smith, M. (2009) *Building Better Behaviour in the Early Years*. London: SAGE.

Goleman, D. (1998) *Working with Emotional Intelligence*. London: Bloomsbury.

Gray, C. and MacBlain, S. (2012) *Learning Theories in Childhood*. London: SAGE.

Miller, L. and Pound, L. (2011) *Theories and Approaches to Learning in the Early Years*. London: SAGE.

Nutbrown, C. (2006) *Threads of Thinking: Young Children's Learning and the Role of Early Education*. London: SAGE.

Rayna, S. and Laevers, F. (2013) *Understanding the Under 3s and the Implications for Education*. London: Routledge.

Visser, J. (2007) *Supporting Personal, Social and Emotional Development*. Everything Early Years How to ... series. London: Everything Early Years.

Parent file

Supporting personal, social and emotional development

- If needed, cut a corner off a comfort blanket so that your child can keep it in their pocket and take to pre-school with them (remember to discuss this with your key person).

- When you're out and about or when walking to pre-school make the most of the time by chatting and pointing things out along the way.

- If you have the time, allow your child to 'dawdle' and notice things around them.

- Introduce a simple routine that includes a 'one-on-one' time with your child, this can be sharing a book or listening to a story tape or just sitting having a cuddle!

- Encourage your child to play with you or other family members but remember and recognise that perhaps your child will still like to play by themselves.

- Offer simple choices to your child, e.g. 'would you like to sit here or there?' as this lets the child know their view or feelings matter to you.

- Keep a special toy/activity to give to your child when you know you need to talk on the telephone or meet with another adult.

- Try to avoid a tantrum or emotional outburst by noticing when these are likely to happen; if one happens do not panic, try to distract your child, keep everyone safe and move on quickly from the incident.

- Be sensitive to your child's feelings, try not to laugh at (even in a good-humoured way) or draw attention to a child's discomfort.

- Try not to put yourself in situations where your child has to wait around for a long time; if it cannot be avoided remember to take snacks and something for your child to do.

- Acknowledge a child's fears without 'talking it up', try to take the panic out of a fear by talking about it in a normal way and saying that everyone gets scared some of the time.

- Anticipate times of worry for your child and prepare them for any changes at home or in your routine.

6

Dealing with feelings and behaviours

This chapter includes:

- **an overview of feelings and behaviour;**
- **appropriate expectations;**
- **focus on practice;**
- **further reflection: theories and trends;**
- **further reading;**
- **Parent file: tantrums and emotional outbursts.**

An Overview

Once safe and secure in their early years setting young children can begin to understand and work through legitimate and varied emotions. Children's behaviour is driven by thoughts and emotions, and when reflecting on any changes to a child's behaviour it is worth remembering that behaviour always originates in an emotion or feeling. Behaviours can be viewed as communication and young children will look to supportive adults to help them make sense of and manage those feelings and any resulting behaviours.

In order to support children to deal with their feelings, practitioners should reflect on children in a holistic way. Considering a child holistically means thinking about the child in their own world. Children do not make the distinction between their feelings at home or within a setting, it is just how they feel. Practitioners can support young children to begin to deal with their feelings by acknowledging and then allowing children to discuss their feelings and emotions. Two year olds are usually not articulate enough to describe their emotions and rely on sympathetic adults to help them label and interpret their mood.

Like adults young children are individuals and some may cope better than others. Once again the adult role is to support them to find ways to begin to understand and deal with their responses.

Some of the emotions children may experience could include:

Emotions young children may feel or experience

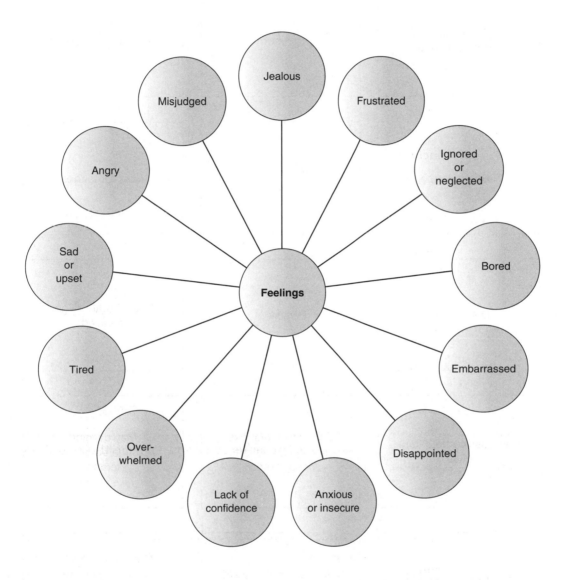

Some common traits that may be seen in two year olds

These traits will be familiar to practitioners who work with two year olds and are part of typical development

Emotionally temperamental	Stubborn	Rigid about routines
Likes to laugh	Can try to dominate adults	Looks for fairness
Demanding	Persistent	Doesn't want to get dressed
Possessive about care giver	Develops fears, e.g. monsters, bedtime, loud noises	May develop nightmares or night terrors
Can be 'over the top' hugging etc.	Can push self forward in a rush to try out new experiences 'my turn'	Cries easily and at times may seem sensitive or embarrassed or overwhelmed

Focus on practice

Practitioners need to feel confident that they can deal with a variety of events and situations in a calm professional, way so that they can support young children to begin to manage their own feelings and emotions.

Find outlined below a range of well tried and tested everyday strategies that practitioners can use to both support children and to develop the skills to be confident in their own practice.

Offering choices

The youngest children can be unpredictable and prone to emotional outbursts even in the warmest emotional environment. One of the most significant strategies to enable the youngest children to develop autonomy and a well-balanced disposition is to support them to make choices. Choice-making empowers children as it makes them feel that they have a say in what they are doing. This is important to all children and especially to those who are very young and striving to be independent

Offering choices means a child is encouraged to select an object or an activity from two or more options. for example, 'What book would you like me to read, Winnie the Poo or Brown Bear?', 'Would you like to play in the sand or in the water?'

It is a useful tool because:

- making choices is a life skill that all children need to learn;
- it avoids conflict over small matters and supports those children who may make a fuss over small things, for example, the colour of a cup;
- young children are more likely to participate when given a choice between two options;
- it supports those children who find selecting activities difficult;
- it allows children to have a say in the day-to-day running of a setting;
- it gives children choices and gives them a way out of a difficult situation.

> ### Example
>
> Sarah didn't want to come and join her friends for 'together time'. Her key worker Mary calmly gestured and said to Sarah 'Sarah, would you like to sit on my knee or on the red cushion?'
>
> Sarah chose to sit on the red cushion.
>
> The situation was resolved quickly as Sarah was supported to make a choice.

Promote children's independence

We have all heard children say 'I do', 'I can', 'Let me do it', 'I wanted to do that!' This is because young children have a strong desire to become independent.

Young children have a right to independence in the same way we all do. Those children who are encouraged to be independent are less likely to become frustrated and will as a result, behave better.

Allow children to 'have a go' and give them time to persevere.

Practice planned ignoring

Sometimes it is best to 'planned ignore' this often diffuses a situation and gives the child time to make a 'sound decision'.

Remember only to use this strategy if the child, or other children, are not likely to come to any harm.

Example

During an outside activity Reuben was seen to be in the corner pushing the duplo off a work bench onto the ground. Farhana, his key worker, was busy with the other children making kites. Farhana continued with the activity ignoring Reuben.

When the children had made their kites Farhana said 'Let's all go into the big garden to run with our kites'. On hearing this Reuben rejoined the group. Farhana let Reuben use the spare kite she had made. The children all enjoyed running in the wind.

After the activity Farhana took Reuben's hand and, while still chatting about the activity, started picking up the duplo pieces, and she said 'Can you help me please Reuben?' and together they cleared up the duplo.

Distraction

To use distraction practitioners need to have a good overview of what is happening in the room.

This strategy is particularly useful in supporting children to avoid confrontation with their peers and to help them to share and play together.

Example

Tom and another child both wanted to use the same doll and buggy. Reena, a practitioner, could see that the other child was engrossed in her imaginative play and the buggy was an integral part of her activity.

On seeing what is about to happen Reena, says in an excited voice, 'Oh look Tom the garage is free let's play'.

When the other child finished with the doll and buggy Reena offered it to Tom and said 'Would you like a turn now?'.

Remove from a potential situation

Sometimes a whole situation can be avoided by simply removing children from a potential upset.

Example

While on a nursery trip to the zoo Rhia, a key worker, was leading a small group. It was almost lunchtime and the children were going to have a picnic. Rhia noticed that there was an ice-cream vendor further down the path; none of the children had yet noticed. To avoid any situation arising, Rhia simply led her group down a different path avoiding the potential conflict.

Try not to always resolve disputes between children

Be a facilitator between children and try not to sort all conflicts out for children (this encourages the beginning of compromise and negotiation). Always try to show children that you recognise their feelings during any disputes, for example, 'I can see that you are upset/angry', as often with two year olds this can be enough to rescue a situation.

Prepare young children for new activities

Thoughtful preparation for new activities can relieve the anxiety for children and, for some, will provide them with the positive attention they need at an appropriate time.

Model the desired behaviour

Show the child what to do as well as saying it.

Example

During tidy up time Tina, a key worker, would always struggle to get Luke to participate and help. Tina asked Luke to help her tidy away the cars; she did most of the tidying while Luke watched her. Tina managed to get Luke to put the last two cars away, praised Luke's efforts and thanked him for his help.

Children will repeat behaviour that receives a positive response.

Photo 6.1   Seeing how far the wheel will roll

Adults as role models

Children learn from those adults around them, therefore practitioners are best placed to show children what positive behaviours look like. Adults who are courteous towards each other provide excellent role models for young children.

It is the responsibility of the manager to ensure that all setting staff maintain the highest standards. Remember, young children learn through observation and doing, and they are observing practitioner interactions all day.

Be consistent

All staff need to do the same thing as consistency is the key to making young children feel safe and secure. Children need to know what is expected of them and all staff also need to have agreed these expectations and how they can best support even the youngest children to manage their feelings and behaviour.

Be seen to be fair

Children need to see fairness happening – to do this successfully a consistent approach needs to be used with *all* of the children. Practitioners should never underestimate how closely children observe staff behaviours. Children learn from those around them and mimic much adult behaviour.

Even the youngest children are passionate about fairness, and practitioners can ensure equality by thinking about some of the points outlined below:

- Do not make promises to children or parents that you cannot keep.

- Try not to show favouritism.

- Be generous and equal with your time.

- Try to facilitate and not referee.

Resist the temptation to bargain

Do not over-complicate interactions with a child by being drawn into bargaining with them, for example, 'If you do this, you can' … conversations. Remember that being consistent and clear is paramount to making children feel at ease and secure. If you feel you want to reward a child that is fine but try not to use the potential reward as a bribe to get a child to do something.

Adults communicating with children

Communicate face to face

When talking to, and especially when checking or correcting a child's actions, bend down and ensure face-to-face contact before speaking. (*Note*: this does not necessarily mean direct eye contact.)

Several things are achieved when you take the time to do this:

- You are giving the child individual attention, which is possibly what he or she needs at that moment in time.

- You are able to ensure the child has heard and understands what you are saying.

Keep language simple

When issuing an instruction, or explaining something to a child, try to keep your language as simple as possible. If in doubt 'check out' what you have said to the child to make sure he or she understands. If you think the child has not understood, rephrase what you have said. Similarly, do not feel you have to give an explanation for everything – keep things simple.

Acknowledge children's feelings

When a child is cross, angry or sad always try to acknowledge how they are feeling. This shows that you are sympathetic and 'tuned in'. This acknowledgement often goes a long way to calming a child down.

> ### Example
>
> Following an upset, Billy got very cross with one of the practitioners. He yelled and screamed and tried to hit her. Jess, his key worker, went over to help. She held Billy gently and said 'I can see that you are very angry right now'. This acknowledgement helped Billy calm down.
>
> *Note*: Jess did not agree with Billy's actions but she did recognise his emotions.

Talking about feelings and behaviour after the event

When children are upset, angry or distressed and the practitioner has acknowledged the feeling, it is often best not to probe and over analyse the behaviour that has just happened. Once a child is cross or upset they often feel 'flooded' with an emotion. While flooded, a two year old may need time and space to calm down and feel more 'balanced'.

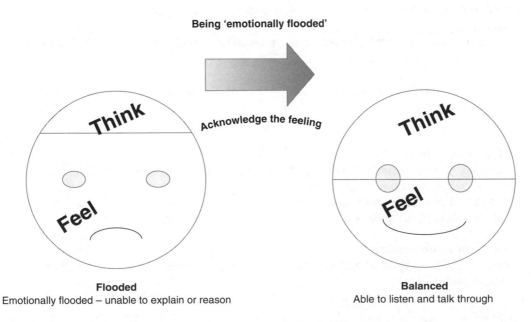

Figure 6.1 Being 'emotionally flooded'

Depersonalise situations that need to be talked about

Young children relate much better when talk is generalised. Try to talk about the issues that may have been raised by individual incidents, using puppets, persona dolls, story books, role play and together time. Use these times to create scenarios which depersonalises situations and help children to see both how their actions affect and appear to others, it will also go a long way to help children start to develop empathy. A two year old can be a very sensitive little person and often the direct approach will upset or embarrass them.

Adults supporting other adults

Working alongside two year olds can be extremely rewarding for practitioners but at the same time it can be exhausting and will require skill and stamina so the adults in the setting need to support each other.

Some ways to do this include:

- After any difficult episode try to build a reflection time at the end of your session, even if it only lasts for 5–10 minutes. It is good to have time to reflect and debrief about what has happened, how it happened and, importantly, how it can be avoided in the future.

- Show a united front and support each other, working as a team and backing each other up. This lets children know that what every member of staff says matters.

Further reflection: theories and trends

Developments in neuroscience and psychological research Many of these support the idea of a child's developing 'theory of mind' and the importance of emotions in learning. Provides some insight into how young children can be supported to self-regulate their emotions and also become independent learners.	Brown and Dunn
Other research highlights differences between girls' and boys' brain development and behaviours.	M. Gurian
Links with the ideas of emotional intelligence and multiple intelligences.	D. Goleman H. Gardner
Behaviourism An early 'learning theory' based on the premise that all behaviours are acquired through conditioning. **Classical conditioning**, describes the learner as passive and learning based on an association between a stimulus and a response.	Ivan Pavlov John B. Watson
Operant conditioning, the learner as an active participant, describes 'The law of effect', an idea that rewards or punishments shape behaviour.	Edward Thorndike B. F. Skinner

Figure 6.2

Further reading

Arnold, C. (2011) *Understanding Schemas and Emotion in Early Childhood*. London: SAGE.

Biddulph, S. (2010) *Raising Boys: Why Boys Are Different*. 3rd edn. London: Harper Thorsons.

Donaldson, M. (1986) *Children's Minds*. London: HarperCollins.

Drifte, C. (2008) *Encouraging Positive Behaviour in the Early Years: A Practical Guide*. 2nd edn. London: SAGE.

Dukes, C. and Smith, M. (2009) *Building Better Behaviour in the Early Years*. London: SAGE.

Gray, C. and MacBlain, S. (2012) *Learning Theories in Childhood*. London: SAGE.

Holland, P. (2003) *We Don't Play With Guns Here: War, Weapon and Superhero Play in the Early Years*. Maidenhead: Open University Press.

Mathieson, K. (2012) *Understanding Behaviour in the Early Years (Early Childhood Essentials)*. London: Practical Pre-School Books.

McTavish, A. (2007) *Feelings and Behaviour: A Creative Approach*. London: Early Education.

Whitebread, D. (2012) *Developmental Psychology and Early Childhood Education*. London: SAGE.

Parent file

Tantrums and emotional outbursts

Q. **What is a tantrum?**

A. A tantrum is when a young child, especially those around the age of two or three, lose control of their emotions and cries and screams or shouts. Some children lie on the floor kicking or can throw things, while others may hit and try to bite those around them.

Q. **What causes a tantrum?**

A. Usually the child is frustrated and is unable to explain themselves, or sometimes it is when the child wants something and an adult has said no.

Q. **How does the child feel when having a tantrum?**

A. The child feels out of control, angry and usually scared.

Q. **Are tantrums inevitable?**

A. Sometimes yes, but often they can be anticipated and prevented.

Q. **How can I help my child avoid tantrums?**

A.
- By working out when a tantrum usually happens and changing the situation so they can be avoided.
- By distracting the child before the tantrum gets hold.

Q. **What can I do when my child is having a tantrum?**

A.
- Try not to be overwhelmed and to stay calm and in control.
- Acknowledge your child's feelings, e.g. 'I can see that you are really angry'.
- Try to distract the child.
- Keep your child safe. This may mean, for example, removing other children or furniture away.
- Hold your child if you think that will help (use your judgement here as sometimes it can make things worse).
- Once the tantrum is over, hug your child and remember they have probably frightened themselves.
- After the event, repeat that you could see that they were very angry BUT the tantrum behaviour was unacceptable.
- Sometime later talk about what the child could do the next time they feel the same way.

7

Checking progress at two years old

This chapter includes:

- an overview of assessment and observation;
- observing learning in the three prime areas;
- focus on practice: checking progress and meeting with parents;
- six steps to recognising and planning for individual needs;
- further reflection: theories and trends;
- further reading;
- Parent file: a two year olds' progress check.

When considering observation and progress for two year olds the main focus will be on the prime areas of learning, that is, personal, social and emotional development, communication and language and physical development. Equally important are young children's attitude, disposition and engagement with learning, which must also be observed in order to encourage and plan for. Sharing these observations and plans with parents and creating a shared understanding is the key to successful partnership working and positive outcomes for children. The whole cycle can be built into the everyday practice of a setting and does not only have to be undertaken at two years of age but can be viewed as good practice at any time, as a way of involving and informing parents, recording progress and moving children's learning on.

Observation

Observation is the single most powerful tool that practitioners have by which to gather information about a young child and to develop their own good practice. It can inform about a child's development and areas of strength, their attitudes and disposition, and how they learn. Observation can begin to give insight into their developing personality and behaviour and help to pinpoint any early needs or difficulties.

Once these observations are put together with all the other information about a child, a more holistic picture emerges and practitioners can begin to analyse, reflect and plan to best support the individual child. Observations can also be enormously helpful in evaluating the environment, resources and practice within a staff team or setting. Lastly, observations also provide a framework, evidence and opportunities to discuss learning with both parents and the children themselves.

Early years practitioners are now very familiar with ongoing formative assessments using notebooks, Post-its, photographs, samples of work or learning stories. These are a purposeful part of everyday practice and form the basis of the 'observe, assess and plan' cycle. There is, however, a skill to observation which only comes with practice. All practitioners need to have the opportunity to carry out extended and different types of observations to ensure that they develop this important skill.

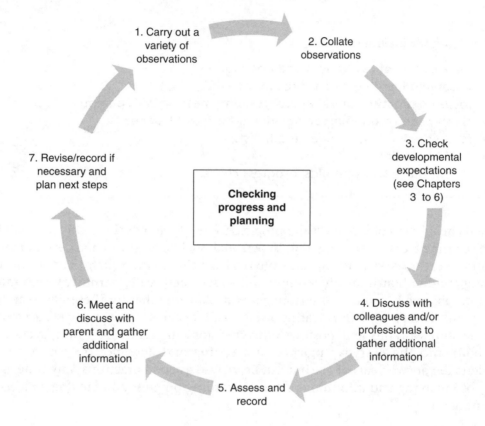

When carried out well and regularly, checking most children's progress at any given point in a summative assessment will be just one part of this ongoing process. For some children, general observations and subsequent discussions with colleagues and parents may raise the possibility of a need or delay in a particular area. This is an opportunity to intervene early and give more focused support. These children will need further specific observations, more targeted or detailed planning of activities, and may need resources and staff support in order to aid their development. In a few cases it may be felt that the child may need further assessment or support and the setting may need to seek additional advice.

Some two year olds may already have some identified additional or special needs when they arrive at your setting. The assessment process for these children should be the same as any other, with a continuous cycle of observation, assessment and planning. In addition, however, you will need to:

- liaise with the professionals already involved with the child, such as speech and language therapist or specialist/advisory teachers;

- consider their stage of development in different areas, which may vary considerably from what might be expected of a child in their age range;

- be aware that progress may be made in smaller steps;

- be sensitive to parents and their feelings about their child's needs.

Observing learning in the three prime areas

In some cases it can be difficult to break down and explain to colleagues or parents what we observe. It can therefore be helpful to have a list of questions to ask yourself after an observation to help analyse what you have seen and heard.

Now follow short lists of guiding questions and prompts to help assess, identify next steps and plan for each of the three prime areas of learning.

Some types of observations

Structured

Particular focus on activities, behaviours or events

Semi-structured

A clear focus but open method

Unstructured

Events recorded as and when they happen

Narratives

A running record of events or single descriptive account

Sampling

Time sampling or event sampling
How often and for how long

Checklists

These should be used with caution

Rating scales

Graphic or numerical records of particular areas of development or behaviours

Diagrams and graphs

These include tracking to measure time and frequency at activities and sociograms to observe social development and interaction

Learning stories

Storytelling to describe a child's learning and thinking process

Language and communication development
Guiding questions and prompts for observation

How?
How did they communicate?
E.g. was it babbling or was the speech clear, did the child use gesture, facial expression, signs?
Did they change their tone of voice or pitch?

Who?
To whom did the child speak? With whom did they interact?
E.g. practitioner or peer/individual or group?

What?
What did they actually *say* or *do*?
E.g. did they use babble, words, phrases, sentences, questions?
What did they *understand*?
E.g. did they follow an instruction, answer a question or comply with a simple request?
Were they able to listen/share attention?

Where?
Where did this take place/the context?
E.g. in the home corner with two other children/outside/story time, etc.

When?
When did they speak?
E.g. were they initiating interaction, answering, talking alongside or commenting to themselves?

Why?
What was the purpose of the interaction and were they successful in their aim?
E.g. were they trying to join in with another child's play or expressing a need?

If not, why not?
What was the reason the child was unsuccessful in their communication?
E.g. they were not understood or did not understand, too quiet, did not have the vocabulary, etc.

Was the child's ability within the range of what is developmentally appropriate?
E.g. was age appropriate, below or exceed expectations?

Physical development
Guiding questions and prompts for observation

What did the child do?
E.g. Gross motor
Climbed on the climbing frame, went around the road track
Avoided the balance beams
E.g. Fine motor
Cutting and sticking activity
E.g. Self-care
Fed themselves yoghurt

What equipment did the child choose?
E.g. Gross motor
Ladder, slide, tricycle or scooter
E.g. Fine motor
Scissors and glue stick
E.g. Self-care
Used a spoon

How did they use the equipment?
E.g. Gross motor
Went up the ladder one rung at a time with right leg leading
Held on to the side of the slide not the rungs
E.g. Fine motor
Changed scissor hands frequently
Tore the paper rather than cut, could not twist the glue stick up
E.g. Self-care
Used mainly right hand, sometimes missed mouth

What was the child's attitude to the activity?
E.g. Gross motor
Very hesitant, constantly looked for help. Got very frustrated
E.g. Fine motor
Reluctant to participate needed lots of encouragement
Could concentrate for one minute
E.g. Self-care
Keen/reluctant/needed encouragement to feed themselves

Was the child's ability within the range of what is developmentally appropriate?
E.g. was age appropriate, below or exceed expectations?

Personal, social and emotional development
Guiding questions and prompts for observation

Self-confidence and self-awareness

Do they separate from parent/carer well?
Are they fully settled?
Do they show particular interests/likes/dislikes?
Do they want to do things for themselves?
Are they able to explore and try new experiences/activities with support?
Do they engage in pretend play?
Are they able to make simple choices?

Making relationships

Have they formed a relationship with a key person?
Do they seek reassurance from a familiar adult?
Does the child play alone/alongside?
Beginning to join in with peers/with a familiar adult?
Have they got a special friend?
Are they beginning to be able to recognise what is theirs and what has to be shared?
Are they able to take turns or play co-operatively with support?

Managing feelings and behaviour

Are they aware of and/or concerned by the feelings of other children and adults?
Can they express their own feelings, such as sadness or fear?
Do they become easily frustrated, angry or upset?
How does this show itself?
Are they beginning to respond to boundaries?
Can they follow routines?
How do they cope with change?

Was the child's ability within the range of what is developmentally appropriate?
E.g. was age appropriate, below or exceed expectations?

A progress check at two

There are many ways and suggested formats for recording a child's progress at two years old. We recommend that you look at as many of these *progress check* formats as you can, discuss as a staff team and, with parents, choose to use or adapt any one of these versions. It is important to remember that the record is a 'summative' assessment, a snapshot of the child at a particular point in time. Ideally it should be carried out when the child is closest to two years old and is fully settled at the early years setting. Apart from contributing to the usual cycle of observe, assess and plan, the other main purpose of the progress check is to identify, record and enable early intervention should any delays or difficulties be found.

It is expected that a child's key person would complete the record, in consultation with colleagues and senior staff who may also have observations and insights into a child. Once the observations have been collated they can be considered and discussed alongside the diagrams in Chapters 3 to 6 and in conjunction with the relevant curriculum guidance. After this, a short summary of the child's stage of development can be written and a professional judgement made on whether or not that development falls within the expected range for their age. This will form the basis of the discussion with parents at the progress check meeting and at this point the record could still be regarded as a draft as the parent's contribution may well bring about some revisions.

The progress check meeting is also an opportunity to plan the *next steps* for the child and to consider ways in which they can be supported in their development. It is useful to write the next steps with parents, as shared understanding and planning for how their child can be moved on helps to ensure that home and setting are working together.

Photo 7.1 Making notes and close up observations

Focus on practice

The progress check meeting

The meeting with parents to discuss their child's progress is obviously an important part of this assessment process. Parents have unique knowledge of their child in a variety of situations and circumstances, not just at home where they are often at their most relaxed and happy. Where good relationships, particularly with a key person, have already been established with parents, this meeting will just be one part of an ongoing dialogue. It is, however, worth giving the meeting some prior thought and preparation to ensure that it is a positive experience for all concerned and has the child at its heart.

Apart from being well prepared in a practical sense it is also important for practitioners to prepare themselves. Often it is the first few minutes which set the tone for the rest of a meeting, so how we approach parents, the language that we use, and how welcome and comfortable parents feel can determine how successful and useful the meeting will be. The following points are useful for individual thought or staff discussion.

Respect and a non-judgemental attitude towards families

At the heart of any positive working relationship lies genuine respect for the families of the children in your setting. It recognises that the family and parents in particular are the most important element in a child's life. Being non-judgemental involves thinking positively about parents, regardless of their personal characteristics, child-rearing practices or situation. It requires a practitioner to believe that parents have a fundamental desire to do the best for their child. A non-judgemental and respectful practitioner communicates confidence that the parents are managing often difficult situations well. The main beneficiary of this positive relationship is always the child.

Developing empathy

Empathy involves showing compassion and understanding towards parents. When developing empathy a practitioner must attempt to understand the feelings and experience of the child and the child's parents. The way a parent may be feeling will depend on what is happening in their life and how things are in relation to their child at any given moment in time. The simplest way to do this is for a practitioner to imagine themselves in their place and consider what their feelings and concerns may be in any given situation an of this example is when they are initially leaving their child in your care.

Active listening

Good listening involves listening to what is being said as well as *how* it is being said. Good *active* listening helps avoid any misunderstanding of the message. Some elements of active listening involve reflecting back, pauses and sometimes silence, nodding, good but not oppressive eye contact, controlled body language and the effective use of questions.

Reflecting back what a parent has said

In order to ensure there is a shared understanding of what has been said between practitioners and parents it is useful to get into the habit of summarising the points parents may make. Do this by saying *'Am I right in thinking you are saying ... '* or *'Sorry but can I just clarify that you mean ... '* or any other similar phrase.

Acknowledging a parent's feelings or emotions

Recognising and acknowledging how parents are feeling can immediately give comfort and reassurance, and often deflects a difficult situation. Acknowledging a feeling does not mean you agree, but it does mean you are open to discussion and are aware of how a parent may be feeling.

Reframing

Reframing can sometimes be used by an experienced practitioner to help parents view something in a new and more positive way. This can mean that during an exchange with parents the practitioner can choose to focus on the positive aspects of a situation and give less attention to a negative, or highlight a small step of progress.

For example, when a parent shows disappointment because their child has not yet started eating snacks at the setting, the practitioner can point out progress by saying 'yes but he has started to look at and show interest in what the others are eating', or 'I think this is a positive step in the right direction'.

Confidentiality

Issues of confidentiality may arise once a practitioner becomes party to sensitive and often personal information regarding a child, their parents and the family as a whole. It is the responsibility of the setting manager to devise a system of information-sharing within their setting. Together they should agree who has access to confidential information within the setting.

Positive body language

For all of us body language occurs subconsciously but those subconscious movements often send powerful messages to the person we are talking to. The main point is to be alert and give your full attention to the person you are talking with, have a relaxed open posture and be aware of personal space.

Open-ended questions

Open ended questions encourage people to talk, invite further information and allow parents to express what are their most relevant and important concerns. Effective questioning will help give practitioners insight into a particular child and how their parent may be feeling, and clarify what has been said or done.

Some useful questions and starting points for discussions with parents

- Tell me about ... (child's name)
- What can we do to help ... (for example, to settle in)?
- What types of activities does ... like to do?
- What sorts of things are challenging for ... ?
- What concerns you most about ... coming here every day?
- What types of changes have you noticed since ... started here?
- What can we do to keep you informed about how ... is doing?
- How do you manage toileting at home? Do you think we should do that here?
- What makes ... happy and content?
- Are you confident we are doing enough to meet ... needs?
- Is there anything else that you would like us to know about ... ?

A note on two year <u>health</u> review

A two year progress check and a health check which usually takes place when toddlers are about two years and six months old can each complement and inform the other, so that difficulties can be identified early and support put in place.

Broadly speaking the purpose of a health and development check is to:

- review the child's social, emotional, behavioural and language development;

- offer guidance on behaviour management and the promotion of language development;

- review development and respond to any concerns expressed by the parents regarding their child's physical health, growth, development, hearing and vision;

- offer advice and information on nutrition, healthy eating, exercise and physical activity for all the family;

- detect early any developmental delay, abnormalities, ill health or growth impairments;

- discuss their current level of immunisation and offer catch ups on any missed immunisations;

- raise awareness about dental care, accident prevention, sleep management, toilet training;

- give parents the opportunity to share any worries or concerns;

- respond to concerns by providing sources of parenting advice and family information and signposting to relevant services;

- provide encouragement and support to take up early years education.

As the number of children in early year's settings who are identified as disadvantaged or vulnerable increases, it is very important that practitioners liaise with health-care professionals. The health visitor often has a wealth of knowledge not only about the child, but also the family as a whole and may have tried-and-tested ideas for ways in which they can be supported.

Where children are identified as having health or developmental problems or special educational needs, health visitors can make early referrals to specialist teams, offer advice and invite parents to join parent groups or programmes. These children may enter an early years setting with clearly identified needs and services in place.

Common points of measurement found in two-year health reviews

Social skills & behaviour

- Plays with toys meaningfully and has some make-believe play
- Has little idea of sharing but may be beginning to take turns
- Plays alongside other children rather than with them
- Is possessive of own toys
- Drinks from a cup and is able to feed self with spoon
- Very curious and tries to investigate everything and has no concept of danger
- Temper tantrums when frustrated but easily distracted
- May have toilet awareness, e.g. know when wet or soiled

Communication & hearing

- Is able to name 3–5 pictures or objects
- May have about 50 understandable words and understands more
- Beginning to make little sentences of two words e.g. 'mummy's keys'
- Is able to tell you what he/she needs
- Is able to carry out simple instruction

Gross motor skills

- Can walk and run without falling over
- Is able to walk up and down stairs holding on and using two feet per step
- Able to throw a ball forward without falling over
- Can walk into a ball to kick it

Fine motor skills

- Builds a tower of 5–6 bricks
- Imitates a circular scribble and straight line
- Able to turn the single pages of a book

Vision

- Recognises pictures of everyday objects, animals etc., in picture books
- No squint seen

Photocopiable:
Provision and Progress for Two Year Olds, © Chris Dukes and Maggie Smith, 2014 (SAGE)

Identifying additional needs

The inclusive nature of early years settings ensures that practitioners will be engaged at some time with children who have a special educational need. Those needs may be identified by practitioners and parents and may be highlighted during the child's attendance at the setting. We have seen that the progress check provides a unique opportunity for practitioners to focus on the developmental needs of individual children and discuss their observational findings with parents. However, practitioners or parents may have concerns at any time about a child.

The six steps diagram on the following page will guide practitioners through a procedure designed to support the identification of additional needs as well as planning for those children who may already be identified.

Referrals and seeking additional advice

For those children who, even with targeted support do not make the progress we would expect or hope for, additional advice often needs to be obtained from professionals with more specialist knowledge. Every local authority or area will have a range of advisers from early years, education and health services and these are accessed differently in each authority.

There is an increasing move towards a more seamless and coherent support for children with special needs and their families. There is recognition of the need to bring both health and education services together to create a co-ordinated provision.

Communicating with other professionals

It is very important to try to liaise with any professional who works with a child in your setting. Children's needs vary between home and early years settings, and practitioners sometimes have different questions and queries from parents regarding individual children. The expertise that a particular professional has can help provide you with specific and focused targets, and their ideas and suggestions can feed into your planning for the child.

Most professionals welcome dialogue with practitioners and their advice can be of huge benefit to the child, but it can also be a time-consuming task which needs mutual perseverance. The following diagram aims to support practitioners to get the best out of any communication.

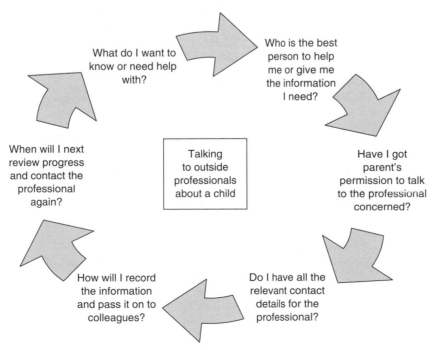

Steps to recognising additional needs

Step 1
A Unique Child – A Holistic View
Think about what you already know
Think about what is happening in the child's life and family circumstances
Talk to parents

Step 2
Enabling Environments – The Reflective Setting
Reflect upon your own setting and practice
What is the child's experience of a day in your nursery?
Are you differentiating and adapting to meet their needs?
Talk to staff

Step 3
Development Matters
Think about what might be developmentally appropriate for the child
Consider their *age* and *stage* of development
Remember every child will develop at a different pace, in different areas, at different times

Step 4
Look, listen and note
Focus on the child's areas of strength and those which are causing concern.
Carry out three or four targeted observations in the area of difficulty.
Try to have more than one person doing the observations
Analyse your observations
What are the most important points you have noted?

Step 5
Plan, Do, Review
Alongside parents decide on a plan of action, this may mean more individualised planning for the child
How can you use the child's strengths?
What needs to be done and who is going to do it?
Regularly review your plan and monitor the child's progress

Step 6
Further advice
If there are still concerns, and with Parental support, seek further advice from outside professional and consider making a referral to a relevant agency such as Speech and Language services or the Community paediatrician

Sources of support

Children's centres

All children's centres will have a wide range of course and groups to support parents. They have outreach workers who can work alongside families and early years settings to help them gain access and liaise with services and support.

Curriculum advisers

These are teachers who can give advice and support on curriculum and planning issues. They will advise on general good practice throughout the setting.

Inclusion adviser/area SENCO

These are teachers or early year's specialists who can advise on inclusion and working with children with special needs. They often have extensive experience or specialist qualifications in working with children with particular needs, such as hearing or visual impairments. Some are involved in direct teaching while others fulfil a more advisory role.

Portage worker

Portage is a home teaching service. It works with children who have special needs, from birth to five years, and their families. Portage workers visit children in their homes on a regular basis to assess and teach new skills. They model the teaching of each skill to enable parents and carers to work with their child in between visits. In this way parents and workers are able to work together, pool their knowledge of the child and support each other. Many authorities have portage workers or those who carry out a similar role.

Educational psychologist

An educational psychologist provides specialist assessment of all kinds of learning. They can give advice on strategies, teaching and learning.

Clinical psychologist

Clinical psychologists work within health service settings. They provide individual and family counselling, family therapy and advice. They can advise and support on a variety of issues including behaviour management and conditions such as autism.

Speech and language therapist

Speech and language therapists will assess, give advice to families and work directly with children who have a speech, language or communication need. They also work with children who have related eating and swallowing difficulties, giving advice on feeding, sucking, food and mouth and tongue movement.

Physiotherapist

Physiotherapists work mainly with children with physical difficulties or delay. They give advice and support, and plan individual programmes which centre on issues such as exercise, co-ordination and balance. They will also advise on specialist equipment like splints, braces, wheelchairs and buggies.

Occupational therapist

Occupational therapists work with children who need help in developing practical life skills because of some form of physical, psychological or social delay or disability. They provide advice and access to specialised equipment, such as chairs, bathing or toileting aids and adaptations to everyday items both at home and in the early years setting.

Community doctors and paediatricians

Doctors and paediatricians work alongside parents to identify and diagnose various illnesses or conditions. They monitor medical conditions as the child grows older and can also refer to other health service professionals.

Health visitors

Health visitors will visit families at home when a child is born and they run various clinics for immunisations, sleep and general development checks. They are available for help, support and advice on all development and health issues.

Social workers

Social workers support children and families in difficult circumstances. They can provide advice and access to other social services provision such as respite care. They will also become involved when there are child protection issues or procedures in place.

Further reflection: theories and trends

A new and still developing multidisciplinary approach to understanding the concept of childhood. Research methods which actively involve children.	The New Social Studies of Childhood (NSSC)
The New Zealand 0–6 curriculum based on sociocultural theory. Four broad principles of holistic development, empowerment, relationships and family and community. Learning stories originated from this curriculum.	Te Whāriki

Figure 7.1

Further reading

Carr, M. (2001) *Assessment in Early Childhood Settings*. London: SAGE.

Carr, M. and Lee, W. (2012) *Learning Stories: Constructing Learner Identities in Early Education*. London: SAGE.

Department of Health (DoH) (2009) *Healthy Child Programme: Pregnancy and the First Five Years of Life*. London: DoH.

Department of Health (DoH) (2009) *Healthy Child Programme: The Two Year Review*. London: DoH.

Dukes, C. and Smith, M. (2009) *Recognising and Planning for Special Needs in the Early Years*. London: SAGE.

Green, C. (2006) *Toddler Taming*. revd edn. London: Vermilion.

Lindon, J. (2012) *Parents as Partners (Positive Relationships in the Early Years)*. London: Practical Pre-School Books.

National Children's Bureau (2012) *A Know How Guide: The EYFS Progress Check at Age Two*. London: NCB.

Hallet, E. (2013) *The Reflective Early Years Practitioner*. London: SAGE.

Kehily, M.J. (ed.) (2004) *An Introduction to Childhood Studies*. Maidenhead: Open University Press.

New Zealand Ministry of Education (1996) *Te Whākiri: Early Childhood Curriculum*. Wellington: Learning Media Ltd.

Nutbrown, C., and Clough, P. (2013) *Inclusion in the Early Years*. London: SAGE.

Palaiologou, I. (2012) *Child Observation for the Early Years*. London: SAGE.

Whalley, M. and the Pen Green Centre Team (2012) *Involving Parents in their Children's Learning*. 2nd edn. London: SAGE.

Recommended websites

www.early-education.org.uk
Learning Together series leaflets.

www.familyandparenting.org
Learning and play booklet.

www.foundationyears.org.uk
Families in the Foundation Years EYFS guide for parents.

Parent file

A two year olds' progress check

Q. **Why have progress checks?**

A. A progress check is a way for staff and parents to monitor a child's development. It is part of the everyday work of all early years' settings, who use the information to identify areas where a child is progressing well and those where progress is at a slower pace than might be expected. In this way it allows earlier identification of development needs so that additional support can be put into place.

Q. **How is my child assessed?**

A. In the early years children's development is assessed through ongoing and continuous observation of your child as they play and learn. There are many kinds of observation which staff will use to see how your child is developing in different areas. As well as observations from the early years setting, you as parents will be asked to contribute to the progress check with the wealth of knowledge that you have about your child.

Q. **What will the check cover?**

A. If your child is aged between two and three years old the check will cover three main or prime areas. These are personal, social and emotional development, physical development and communication and language development. It will also look at the way your child approaches learning and new experiences.

Q. **How will I get the information from the progress check?**

A. You will be asked to attend a meeting at the early years setting. The meeting will almost certainly be led by your child's key person because they will be the practitioner who knows your child the best. Other staff may also have contributed to the observations and information which has been collected and summarised into a draft report. You will have the opportunity to comment, discuss and contribute to this report before it is finalised and sent to you.

Q. **What will happen if my child is not making the progress expected in any areas?**

A. If your child does not seem to be making the progress which might be expected in any area you will be able to plan together with the practitioner for how you can support their development. This will mean planning activities and other opportunities at the setting and at home to move them forward, these are often referred to as 'next steps'. In some cases it may mean accessing additional advice from other professionals such as speech and language therapists.

It is very important to remember that each child is unique. Children develop at different rates at different times in different areas and a child may seem to be more developed in one area than others and periods of rapid development may be followed by a much slower rate of progress. Any progress check will only give a picture of a child at one given point in time.

Index

Admissions 3, 4
Adults as role models 53, 72
Attachment 6, 7, 56

Bandura A. 63
Behaviour 24, 66
Behaviour traits 68
Bronfenbrenner 63
Brown & Dunn 74
Bruner 20

Characteristics of effective learning
    12, 13–16
Checking progress 31
Commenting 31

Emotional environment 56
Emotionally flooded 73
Emotional security 62
English as an Additional Language 35
Environment 18, 19

Feelings 66, 67, 73
Fine Motor Skills 44–45, 46, 52
Food and eating 47–48
Forest Schools 53
Froebel F. 53

Gardiner H. 74
Giving choices 32
Goleman D. 74
Gross Motor Skills 40–41, 42, 43
Gurian M. 74
Gussin-Paley V. 35

Highscope 20
Holistic 57
Home visits 4

Identifying additional needs 89, 90

Jarman E. 35

Keyperson 5, 6, 57
Kodàly 35

Laevers F. 63
Laevers & Moon 63
Language development:
    expressive language 26, 29
    pace of development 24,

Language development cont.
    receptive language 25, 28,
    vocabulary spurts 23,

Makaton 35
McMillan R. & M. 53
Modelling 31
Montessori M. 53.

New Social Studies of Childhood (NSSC) 92

Observations 77, 79, 80, 81, 82, 83
Offering choices 32, 69, 14

Parents 1–3, 8–9, 57
Parents File 10, 22, 37, 55, 65, 76, 94
Pavlov I. 74
Personal social and emotional development
    58, 59
Physical activity 38–39, 40, 52
Physical literacy 38
Piaget J. 20
Progress check 84, 85, 94
Progress and planning 78

Reggio Emilia 20
Resilience 57
Routines 20–21

Schemas 27
Self-care 47, 49, 50
Signalong 35
Skinner B. F. 74
Soothers (dummies) 27
Sources of support 91, 92
Speech and language therapist 24
Stammering 30
Steiner Waldorf 53

Tantrums 76
Te Whāriki 92
Thorndike E. 74
Toileting 48
Turn taking 32, 63
Two year health review 87, 88

Verbal prompts 32
Visual prompts 32
Vygotsky L. 20

Watson J.B. 74

978-1-4462-0766-6

978-1-4462-0924-0

978-1-4462-1109-0

978-1-4462-0708-6

978-0-85702-535-7

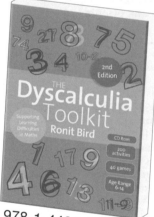
978-1-4462-6719-6

978-1-4462-6023-4

Find out more about these titles and our wide range of books for education practitioners at **www.sagepub.co.uk/education**

978-1-4462-1075-8

978-1-4462-0283-8

978-1-4462-4913-0

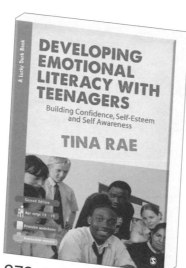

978-1-4462-4915-4

978-0-85702-167-0

Find out more about these titles and our wide range of books for education practitioners at **www.sagepub.co.uk/education**

EXCITING TITLES ON BEHAVIOUR MANAGEMENT FROM SAGE